THE GREAT COMMUNION REVIVAL

DEAN BRIGGS

KANSAS CITY, MO

The Great Communion Revival

Copyright © 2023 by Dean Briggs
Published by Champion Press
Kansas City, MO

All rights reserved. Except for brief quotations in printed reviews, no part of this publication may be reproduced, stored in a retrieval system, or transmitted in any form or by any means (printed, written, photocopied, visual electronic, audio, or otherwise) without the prior permission of the publisher.

Unless otherwise indicated, all other Scripture quotations are from the The Holy Bible, English Standard Version® (ESV®), copyright © 2001 by Crossway, a publishing ministry of Good News Publishers. Used by permission. All rights reserved.

Scripture quotations also include NEW AMERICAN STANDARD BIBLE®, Copyright © 1960, 1962, 1963, 1968, 1971, 1972, 1973, 1975, 1977, 1995 by The Lockman Foundation.

Scripture taken from The Message. Copyright © 1993, 1994, 1995, 1996, 2000, 2001, 2002. Used by permission of NavPress Publishing

Scripture taken from Authorized King James Version (KJV) is public domain.

Cover and book design: Barkley & Co.
Editors: Barbara Sisti, Jeanie Briggs

ISBN-13: 979-8393140526

First Edition – May 2023
Printed in the United States of America

Other Books by Dean

NON-FICTION

- *Ekklesia Rising*
- *Consumed: 40 Days of Fasting & Rebirth*
- *The Jesus Fast* (co-authored with Lou Engle)
- *Longhairs Rising*
- *Brave Quest: A Boy's Journey to Manhood*
- *The Total Superiority of the New Covenant*
- *The Power of Your New Creation Life*
- *The Calling & Purpose of the Ekklesia*
- *Partakers of the Divine, Pt. 1 & 2*

FICTION (under D. Barkley Briggs)

- *The Legends of Karac Tor* (5 Books)
- *The Withering Tree*
- *The God Spot*
- *The Most Important Little Boy in the World*

TABLE *of* CONTENTS

Author's Note

Introduction

WHISPERS & DREAMS

1   Dreaming of Revival
2   Judging the Powers
       Excursus A: Theology of Spiritual Warfare
3   A Door Opens

BETTER THINGS

4   A Template for Better Revival
       Excursus B: Edenic Fellowship Restored
5   Passover Decade & Prophetic Activism
6   The Shield Wall of History

BETTER BLOOD

7   Inheritance, Markers & Signs
8   The Final Blood Line of History
9   Overcoming the Accuser
       Excursus C: The Experience of Divine Love
10   The Divine Meal

THE LAMB WAVE

11   The Lamb Wave
12   Global Communion

End Notes

AUTHOR'S NOTE

For those who take time to read an Author's Note, I must explain the origins of this book. I do so with confidence that God will touch you in its pages, but also with a bit of remorse for the convoluted process it took to get to this point.

Sadly, the first edition was written on an unrealistic, self-imposed deadline. In fact, I had no intention of writing this book at all. Then, after 2-3 years of pondering the prophetic narrative you are about to read, I found myself scheduled to speak at a conference in February of 2022. The topic was going to be centered on the very idea this book explores, that a "great communion revival" was beginning, or perhaps even *had* begun. I felt an unavoidable inner prompting to commit to both starting and finishing my book in time for that event, even though there was little time.

As an author of several books, the idea of a "rush job" ran contrary to my finicky inner editor. I normally insist on a well-manicured, thoroughly vetted manuscript that is thoughtfully developed, clean and polished. I don't like mistakes, nor rewrites; certainly not *after* publication! In this instance, however, I felt it was more important to have the book ready to distribute at the February conference even if further work remained.

Warily, but knowingly, I rushed the first version out the door to make the deadline, only to immediately recognize things that should have been cut and others that should have been added. In the few intervening months since that first edition, more pieces of the puzzle have emerged.

Even the title is no longer as appropriate as it once seemed. In my travels, I have seen evidence that, instead of *The Coming Great Blood Communion Revival*, the more appropriate title is simply, *The Great Communion Revival*.

Why? Because though a fledgling movement at present, I believe it has already begun.

While humbling to release my "work in progress" on a wide scale, I felt it to be a matter of obedience in my soul. For those who purchased the original version, I now humbly and apologetically release what I consider to be the correct version – which the best and truest in message and form.

I assure you, this is personally too embarrassing to be a sales ploy. In Section 2 alone, I consolidated three chapters on Leviticus to one, permitting two additional chapters with more dreams and biblical insights that hew more closely to the topic of Communion itself. The removed portions remain critical to a better understanding of the old covenant versus new, yet it became clear they belonged to a different work because they tended to break the flow and focus of *this* work.

Add in a number of minor corrections throughout and the changes are now substantive enough, resulting in a more unified work, to justify the new edition you hold in your hands.

Dean Briggs
May 1, 2023

INTRODUCTION

At a fundamental level, the Bible is a story of kingdoms in conflict. Equally, it is the story of God's total, relentless commitment to full fellowship with man in the overflow of divine love. The story of God is therefore one of love conquering hate, and good overcoming evil. From eternity to now, the war against Satan is perhaps one of the most important frameworks by which we comprehend our redemption.

The building blocks of this epic story are both historically actualized and symbolically codified in the vernacular of Scripture. We have been given history, poetry, wisdom, narrative and a codebook of divine, infallible inspiration from which we are meant to continually draw riches deep and new, old and true. Blood is one such code, operating on many levels. It is both real and symbolic. Blood is typological, medical, historical, and salvific. Another truth, both real and veiled in code, is contained in the ritual of covenant. Sacrifice is yet another. By these we better glimpse God's redemptive agency toward humanity because they all prophesy or proclaim Christ.[1]

Some might be surprised to discover that Communion is one of the most potent yet overlooked realities in the lexicon of grace.

Its potency lies in the fact that the experience of the bread and wine forms a convergence point of every symbol mentioned above, and more besides.

This is a book about Communion. It is aspirational, in that I am reaching for things I glimpse in Scripture, yet long to more fully experience. It is prophetic in that I believe the message of this book is forward-thinking and proclamatory, not only of God's past design, but also His future intent. It is inspirational in that any book about Communion would do well first to recognize that God's desire to commune with us lies behind any theology that might follow of the possibility of man communing with Him.

This is, therefore, a book about war, love and redemption, or more specifically, their practical intersection when we partake of the body and blood of Christ. Many others have addressed the devotional aspects or theological quandaries arising from the execution of Communion. My gaze is not upon ecclesiastical protocol, or systematic theology, but upon the mystery of Christ; in particular, truths that might have gotten lost among Protestants along the way, and how the recovery of those things might be eschatologically incumbent upon us to regain.

Through a series of short, colorful explorations, in wave after wave, I hope to reacquaint the reader with a biblical view of blood in such a manner that our practice of Communion would correspondingly enlarge. Even now I believe the Spirit is whispering similar things to many others around the world as part of the Father's great plan to culminate history in adoration of His glorious, beautiful Son.

For all these reasons, almost of necessity, this is also a book of dreams. What do I mean? Consider first what it means to be the *imago dei.* That little Latin phrase packs a wallop by compacting the truth of Genesis 1 into two little words. It means that humans are made in the *image* of *God*.

To be the *imago dei* is to confess in agreement with the Word that men and women are designed by God to embody Him in countless, creative ways. While the present manifestations of our "imaging of God" reveal and reflect our Creator magnificently enough, our full potential must surely be staggering. As an example, could *imago dei* not suggest that the human capacity to dream (daydream and night dream) correlates roughly to those unfathomable, internal desires by which the Godhead manifests His plan over time?

Of course, God does not dream in the sense that He has unfulfilled longings, or visions in the night, or is working through anxiety in His soul. But as the sovereign architect of history, He does have a *purpose* that remains largely veiled to man. His omniscient knowledge includes a divine plan by which mysterious goals are slowly being realized in time and space. His plan isn't constructed of bullet points on a Powerpoint, it's revealed in *story* with a plot and unique characters. There is struggle, darkness, danger and triumph. Thus, the story of God hides the mind of God in whispers, symbols and layers.

How do humans exhibit this mysterious quality of God? Again, if that faculty were to be embodied in some wondrous human capacity, however diluted, would it not almost seem like our magical ability to dream? Scientific studies have concluded that we have about two thousand daydreams per day, each averaging fourteen seconds.[2] Why do we do this?

Do our dreams not come to us, almost unbidden, as mysteries of vivid color, hidden purpose, and rich symbolism? Do they not inevitably seem to weigh on our souls with purpose and promise? Do they not whisper strange tales, as if transplanted into our subconscious from another world, as inscrutable frequencies from a faraway land, perceivable only when our rational mind finally becomes subordinate to our spirit in the state of rest? Do dreams not sometimes, perchance, inform our steps, guide our ambitions, and warn our ways, urging us to become more deeply a part of God's fantastical plan?

Indeed, how could our dreams not be fantastical if we are made in His image and His plan is fantastic?

Thus, if we understand God's "dream" to represent His own desired outcome, which He will relentlessly and inexorably achieve, for what does God dream?

Thankfully, we see His desire spelled out in Scripture. From start to finish, God's great longing is to have a people who will love Him as much as He loves them, and to fellowship with that people in unfettered, unbroken joy.

Because evil entered the plot, threatening to cripple that people and steal that joy, an invisible battle of love lurks behind the veil of history. As in any battle, every advantage matters. No one wants to limit their options if victory is at stake. Similarly, in battle, every person must eventually choose a side. So it is that the earth is coming to a point of no return, an irrevocable point of final decision.

Lines are being drawn. Choices are being made. Power is being tragically utilized; or, sadly, within the church, not at all.

> "**Multitudes, multitudes, in the valley of decision! For the day of the LORD is near in the valley of decision.**" (Joel 3:14)

Just as Jesus predicted, the fine wheat of the Kingdom and the false tares of the wicked are simultaneously ripening toward full maturity at the end of the age. Earth's atmosphere and the cultures of man are becoming increasingly entwined, spiritual in their longing, and correspondingly irreligious and pagan in their pursuit. Orthodoxy is rapidly faltering, while syncretism, magic and ritualism are on the rise. People are looking for experiences to fill the rapidly expanding void brought on by a sugar-coated, narcissistic, technology-driven value system that thinks it has successfully killed God, only to find themselves drowning in the terrible existential despair of any world where God is not.

That world has a name: hell.

More than ever, the *imago dei* cannot help but long for communion with *something*. Anything. And therein lies the terrible danger of this hour of human history.

Indeed, lines are being drawn.

Perhaps some of these themes seem too grand, or theatrical, or abstract, so let me frame it more simply. At the most rudimentary level, if Communion holds power, I don't want to be left holding the short straw simply because I refused to contemplate its mysteries. If Communion is more than a symbol, I do not want to treat it only as a symbol. Nor, I think, do you, though that specific thought might have never occurred to you. However, if you feel roughly the same, I propose we start as lowly and humbly as possible.

Since I assume my audience is mostly comprised of some flavor of Evangelicalism, here's a thought that might trouble you, but is worth asking nonetheless: what do Catholics know that we, perhaps, do not? Maybe they are wrong, but maybe they are more right than we have wanted to admit. Or maybe, even if we are more right, could their understanding still enlarge our world?

I don't want to merely be right, I want to fully commune with Christ in *this* life, not just the life beyond.

Could it be that the Reformation, in all its righteous zeal, accidentally threw out a couple of really important babies with the bathwater? If that's too hard to swallow, then maybe try this: as a Protestant, whether Evangelical, charismatic or mainline, could we have the humility to admit that most of us have simply not been trained in the possibility of *knowing God more through Communion,* even though that is the very essence of the word?

Instead, whether by habit, teaching or a certain degree of convenient neglect, we were basically shown that Communion is not unlike a period at the end of a sentence. It's small, doesn't take up much space or attention in our normal routine, and mainly serves to let us know that the more important thought expressed by the sentence itself is now finished. In other words, Jesus wrote the sentence with His life and death, then basically handed us bread and wine with a perfunctory appeal: "Just try to remember, okay?"

In all sincerity, I assure you I do not mean to be flippant in that description. Quite the opposite, I want to draw our attention to the problem of how flippant we have already been! Can we start there and admit that if the problem is real, a solution is needed? As stated, it is not my purpose to argue the history of the Reformation, the various possible errors of Roman Catholic doctrine that led up to it, or to parse heady theological terms like *transubstantiation* as compared to *consubstantiation*.

I simply want to rediscover the spiritual potency of the blood of Jesus, and to better recognize the Bible's dreamlike hints of that potency embodied in Old Testament rituals. Furthermore, I want to embrace the manner in which the new covenant redefines those symbols into living reality. Then, from that hopeful place, I hope to give voice to a growing movement of *communers*. I truly believe that heaven desires to commune with earth like never before. As such, I hope to articulate why such a movement might be crucial in the desires of God as a matter of eschatological beauty and utility.

If we do not yet understand the full privilege and meaning of Communion in our personal experience, perhaps we should at least contemplate its imperative. The Eucharist, whether as an opportunity for divine fellowship (as a meal you share with God) or as a mission of appropriation and reenactment, is obviously intended to be more than a quick nip of crackers and watery grape juice. It is inherently sacramental, a work of grace. The older I get, the more I realize my great need of grace. How about you?

So as my understanding deepens, I suspect I will see that taking bread and wine as Christ offered them is to value each at a level approaching the incarnational potential of His presence in my life. This is a far cry from most "Communion services." No less an Evangelical stalwart than J.I. Packer said, "Why do Protestants dumb down the Supper? Why do we take for granted, as we seem to do, that it is of secondary and minor importance?"[3]

Indeed, our half-hearted, ADHD, eyes wandering, check-our-watch, quickly-pass-the-plate-and-get-to-the-sermon-tokenism afforded to most Evangelical expressions could hardly qualify as even the merest "remembrance" of Christ in His suffering, much less a divine contemplation of His nearness in the elements.

I know this message will face challenges. Some will welcome it and press in. But to speak of a Blood Communion Revival is to invite sneers from certain sectors of the Body of Christ if for no other reason than because I have placed what some might consider an unnecessary emphasis on dreams as part of the conviction behind the possibility. To those readers, I simply affirm my deep commitment to the Word and to the conviction that Scripture conveys anointing, inspiration and truth far beyond any dream. At the same time, I also must confess that each of the dreams I will share were directly employed by the Holy Spirit to focus our attention *more* on Scripture, not less; and without their prompting, we might have missed beautiful additional revelations embedded in God's *Logos*.

Secondly, such phraseology may invite caution or avoidance from folks who love Jesus but are uncomfortable with too much talk of blood in polite society. These believers may struggle with embarrassment that the primitive roots of our faith will make us seem more superstitious than enlightened in the eyes of the world. I have no easy reply to that. The Bible is what it is. Like it or not, your faith is based on blood.

Finally, other "hardliners" might take theological issue as a matter of principle for fear that any talk of "deeper meaning" or "experience" to the rite of Communion could be accidentally or nefariously inspired by what is perceived to be Roman Catholic error. (This could be particularly sensitive across Europe.)

While I respect that concern, I can't afford to be backed into a corner by it. The older I get, the more I have found that many of our pet doctrines represent strongholds of tradition and pride, which, if true, creates a terrible scenario where God will resist us *even in our rightness*. I would rather choose to learn from those who have walked with Jesus over many years and loved Him greatly, whether they fit my tradition or not. The total portrait of Communion, painted so beautifully over countless centuries by such saints, is quite different than the rather perfunctory view common to many of us today.

Ever mindful of our ongoing need for more of Jesus, I am gripped with this idea that God's own dream (full fellowship with man) and literal dreams might one day converge. Such dreams will mark the pages of this book. These dreams connect *blood* and *communion* and *revival* in a powerful, undeniable way.

I say again, I don't want to merely be right, I want full communion with Christ.

I trust that is true of you, as well.

The Great Communion Revival

WHISPERS & DREAMS

chapter 1

DREAMING OF REVIVAL

"HE (God) SPEAKS IN DREAMS, in visions of the night when deep sleep falls on people as they lie in their beds. HE WHISPERS IN THEIR EARS and terrifies them with warnings."

Job 33:15-16

The Great Communion Revival

Nearly twenty years ago, a dream came to one of our most trusted dreamers indicating a future time when something called the "Blood Communion Revival" would begin to spread across the earth. In the dream, a treasure chest buried in the sands of time had opened, and the letters that floated out of it spelled that phrase. The Blood Communion Revival would be a dramatic catalyst, perhaps *the* catalyst, for an unprecedented move of God in the last days.

The dream was chiefly directed toward my friend and mentor, Lou Engle. It was a prophetic word meant to stir vision and faith, something into which Lou was meant to pray and for which he should believe. While the meaning of the dream was obvious in one sense, it was also somewhat veiled. What is a Blood Communion Revival? It wasn't entirely clear. We had the headline, but not the story.

Nevertheless, the vividness and simplicity of the dream had done it's work, depositing a gift of fascination and faith. Over the following two decades, a close knit group of devoted friends, fervent intercessors and glorious comrades took up this same call with Lou, not knowing for certain what it meant or when it would begin to manifest. *(When I speak in the plural as 'we,' I am referring to this community)*.

Twenty years passed with the echo of the dream in our souls, but little else. No new dreams. No further clarity. No sense of what might be next, or when. Year after year, a series of other critical intercessory assignments occupied our time, passion and prayers.

But that phrase – Blood. Communion. Revival. – never fully departed. It inspired our imaginations, our longings.

- **Blood** not only secures salvation, it defines your family line, therefore your sense of identity. Blood carries your DNA. Blood speaks of passion, sacrifice, and covenant, ideas that powerfully converge in the blood of Jesus.

- **Communion** is a word that evokes deep emotion and longing. Communion is intimacy. You cannot commune with a stranger, only the closest of friends, or a lover. Communion is giving and receiving, with union as the prize. To commune does not mean we lose ourselves, only that we become more than ourselves by taking on the qualities of the one with whom we commune.

- **Revival** shapes reality in new ways. Revival is an alarm clock, suddenly rousing the sleeping dead. Revival brings hope, salvation, anointing, conviction, deliverance and power to the lost. It is the thing that happens when the veil thins enough for things to spill over from one world into another. In all of history, there have been precious few true Holy Spirit revivals.

In 2020, to our surprise, even as nations began to convulse politically, medically and morally under the toll (and perhaps the agenda?) of the Covid-19 pandemic, and amidst an accelerated deterioration of social norms, the dreams suddenly resumed. Honestly, we weren't looking for them. Candidly, we might not have been as faithful to the original assignment as we should have been. Nevertheless, as if giant, invisible gears began to turn the clock by which God governs His own agenda for earth, our dreams resumed. We began to hear of others who were having similar dreams. Pro tip: when dreams spontaneously emerge from multiple directions, all bearing the same divine imprimatur, we should take heed.

> "Consciously or unconsciously, one lives not only one's life, but the life of one's time...*Are our dreams, for example, to some degree facets of a larger mass dream that is beginning to happen in the world?*...To put it another way, when God wants to initiate a new movement in history, God does not intervene directly, but sends us dreams and visions that can, if attended to, initiate a process."[4] (italics mine in passages quoted throughout the book)

I take dreams seriously and hope you do, too. I believe God speaks to us much more in our dreams than we typically realize or believe.[5] To neglect our dreams is unbiblical and potentially deleterious to our destiny, so I want to attend to these dreams, not ignore them. If possible, I want to initiate a process, a conversation between you and me and heaven, so we can all hear and judge whether God is collectively "whispering in our ear." To that end, I'll sprinkle several key dreams throughout this booklet. I don't put dreams equal to Scripture, but I do believe Scripture tells us to pay attention to our dreams. It also says to tell others.

> **"*Write the vision*; make it plain . . . so he may run who reads it. For still the vision awaits its appointed time."** (Habakkuk 2:2-3a)

Said Victor Hugo, author of *Les Miserablés*, "There is nothing like a dream to create the future."[6]

Before we can shape the future, we must first soberly appraise our unique moment in history. It is important to consider (and remember) not just the turmoil of the early 2020s, but the history-altering significance those days brought to planet earth. While the genius of God is definitely at work, wisdom demands that we strive for broader perspective if we are to fully appreciate the distinction between what He is actively doing versus passively permitting.

Either way, there is no way around the fact that the world has changed. We are not in a new season, but a new *era*. You would probably have to go back to the Industrial Revolution, or perhaps even further to the Protestant Reformation, to witness a period of equally historic, far-reaching upheaval. Briefly establishing that fact is important to the urgent message of this book.

The Tumultuous 2020s: A New Era Dawns

When China reported the first Covid-19 death on January 11, 2020, it was largely a non-story. This quickly changed. Within two months, the following headlines appeared in major news outlets:

- "Coronavirus Will Change the World Permanently: Here's How" *(Politico)*
- "Coronavirus Ushers in the Globalization We Feared" *(Bloomberg)*
- "COVID-19 Is The Crisis That Will Impact Generation Z's Worldview" *(Forbes)*
- "The Coronavirus Pandemic Will Forever Alter the World Order" *(The Wall Street Journal)*

As these and other headlines began to dominate the news, it was as if two competing agendas were striving to shape the future, and one had nothing to do with revival. The *Wall Street Journal* article went on to call for the "urgent work of planning for a new epoch." These are four of dozens, perhaps hundreds of articles, ranging from scholarly sources, think tanks, magazines, newspapers and other media outlets, both liberal and conservative.

On April 3, 2020, *WSJ* guest columnist Henry Kissinger wrote, "History is accelerating, and the leaders, values, institutions and ideas that guide society are going to be tested severely by the struggles ahead." The sub-headline declared, "The world is entering a transformative era. Prepare for more chaos and instability."[7]

Yet Covid was only part of the story.

In that same period of time, Iran launched its first military satellite and attacked U.S. bases in Iraq. The Abraham Accords were signed (the first time Israel has openly signed any sort of cooperative or "normalization agreement" with an Arab state), inching us forward in biblical prophecy. A massive election controversy transpired in the United States (whichever side of the political spectrum you align with, the nature of the controversy significantly undermined confidence in the world's strongest democracy both at home and abroad).

In 2021, a military coup in Myanmar and North Korea's test of tactical nukes, along with the escalation of tensions between China and Taiwan, brought further instability across east Asia, while in central Asia and Europe, Russia began amassing personnel and equipment on Ukraine's border. Also in 2021, social media and 'Big Tech' publicly began deplatforming conservative voices, censoring dissent, and demonetizing opposition. Many of these voices were often Christian in content or perspective (though often not). In matters of commerce, when the cargo mega ship, *Ever Given,* got stuck in the Suez Canal, the rippling domino effect delayed thousands of other shipments, triggering a global supply chain crisis that further shocked and stressed many Covid-devastated industries.

On the Covid front, masks and social distancing were mandated, followed by increasingly severe fines and even the closure of businesses. Nations followed with vaccine mandates, breaking nearly every major review process and accountability structure previously required for new drug approval. The major economies of the world all but shut down, ostensibly to protect the planet's population from the terrible risk of what would end up claiming .00086 of the global population.

During this period, entire nations were encouraged to leverage themselves into as much debt as necessary to keep operations afloat, which they did. Ever wonder why? It's openly called The Great Reset, and more and more global leaders are buying into the plan. Professor Klaus Schwab, Founder and Executive Chairman of the World Economic Forum, a leading architect for The Great Reset, said this:

"The pandemic represents a rare but narrow window of opportunity to reflect, reimagine, and reset our world."

But resets aren't easy. Eventually, the massive economic toll and social restrictions led to global protests. In Canada, thousands of truckers peacefully flooded the capital in protest, before they were criminalized and forcibly disbanded by the federal government. In America, the dramatic events of the Presidential

Inauguration on January 6 further divided an already embittered electorate. Later that year, President Trump would be impeached and Justice Ruth Bader-Ginsberg would die, paving the way for Amy Coney Barrett, a conservative constitutionalist, to replace her and eventually secure the historic overturn of Roe v. Wade (one year later on the 50th anniversary of the original ruling). Meanwhile, for the first time in history, the Roman Catholic Pope met with the Grand Ayatollah in Iraq at roughly the same time as the United States executed its disastrous pullout of Afghanistan under the direction of President Biden. No surprise, the Taliban swiftly regained power. The pace of global change was dizzying.

But it wasn't over. In 2022, Russia invaded Ukraine. The Sino-Russian axis strengthened, while developing further ties to Islamic states. NATO also strengthened and realigned, triggering nuclear escalations in Russia, Belarus, and Pakistan. News reports declared the southwest USA to be in a 1200-year "megadrought," but this was only one of several global environmental challenges producing fearful speculation of major food shortages in 2023 and beyond.

Circling back to Covid thirty months later, government statistics claimed 443 million cases had occurred globally, including 6 million deaths. The pandemic had shifted to an endemic – our "new normal."

Such a broad and scattered summary of events can hardly be considered complete. I have barely addressed, or ignored, a range of other dire scenarios, including: the rapid normalization of gender fluidity; crisis levels of depression and suicide among teens; the opioid and fentanyl epidemic; frightening surges of totalitarian policies in historic democracies; escalating economic prejudice against moral "non-conformists" (people who stand by their biblical and/or conservative convictions). Much more transpired on the international stage, as well. But let me add one more: 2022 will likely be recorded as the year that Artificial Intelligence (A.I.) became truly viable, promising to reshape the world in unimaginable and terrifying ways. For those that know the reference, Skynet is now alive.

Hindsight is Truly 2020

Ironically, for the first time in history, the old adage about hindsight being 20/20 has taken on literal proportions. Is there hope for the future? In light of this crush of momentous, world-shifting events, how should we contemplate the days ahead?

With a bit of reflection and anointed hindsight, hopefully we can better recognize what God is doing moving forward. I think its fair to say the church missed it in so many ways as we first headed into 2020. Prior to that, over the course of 2019, many leaders were increasingly confident that a radical advance – nay, a divine intrusion – of the next Jesus Movement was imminent. On our doorstep. In my own small way, I was one of them. I was proclaiming that streets and stadiums were going to be filled with evangelism. Instead, by government mandate, those same streets grew utterly silent. Stadiums emptied, not filled. Covid-19 appeared and everyone disappeared. They went home, locked their doors, and stood six feet apart. Neighbors wouldn't talk to each other out of fear. Everything shut down except for the riots.

Instead of mass evangelism, we got mass demonstrations, and a dark new prophetic narrative called "cancel culture." At first, the staccato pace of these bizarre events registered like a dopamine hit for both conservative biblical eschatologists and liberal social justice warriors, i.e. are we *finally* going to see the long overdue, tectonic, culture shifts that will mark the end of the age?

In the short term, you would not be alone to feel quite discouraged. When the church thought zig, God zagged. Across the board it seemed like the church had nothing meaningful to say. We were caught mostly flat-footed, voiceless, nearly as bewildered as everyone else. The 2020s were supposed to represent a bold, high profile gospel advance. Evangelism would be like shooting fish in a barrel. Instead, the decade quickly began to feel more like the proverbial canary in the coal mine, warning us of the imminent collapse of civilization, not revival.

take heart, there's a lot of decade left, a lot of God left, and we've had lessons to learn

Take heart, friends. There's a lot of decade left, a lot of God left, and we've had important lessons to learn, like how to inquire deeply and thoughtfully of the Lord once more; how to trust His leading more than our wisdom or momentum; how to reframe success and throw much of our "surging, booming, glitzy" success narrative out the window in favor of becoming faithful witnesses to His return.

None of the above correctives should be taken to mean that revival is not on God's heart. Quite the opposite, I think the Holy Spirit is so committed to revival that He is recalibrating our small idea to better fit His big idea. He wants us to recognize the *what*, *why* and *how* in which revival will come. While our idea of revival seemed grand to us, it was simply too small, too conventional, and too mundane to truly reflect God's glorious purpose at this stage of human history. We wanted people to get saved, but secretly, we wanted them to get saved *by us*. We wanted our brand, our story, to frame the talking points. We were so focused on so many laudable gospel outcomes that we did not recognize how mixed our motives had become.

Our notion of revival was not only too predictable, it was accidentally rooted in creature comforts. The Holy Spirit is going to move, we said! (by which we meant *it will be easy*). Revival will be awesome! (by which we meant *it will be fun*). The subtle implication was that revival would happen in a way that added to our lives without disrupting our schedules. We didn't say that, but we thought it. The popular concept of revival was exciting, personal and pleasant. It was micro, not macro. It was power, not persecution or pain.

Revelation 12, which we will examine in greater detail in chapter eight, challenges that in the strongest terms. This pivotal chapter says the greatest revival in history – when **"the salvation and the power and the kingdom of our God and the authority of His Christ have come"** (v. 10) – exists in the context of cosmic war, human hatred, and on the continuum between accusation, betrayal, and martyrdom. In that environment, the people of God will conquer **"*by the blood of the Lamb* and *by the word of their testimony*, for they *loved not their lives even unto death*"** (Rev. 12:11).

Read that again. The Body of Christ will *understand*, *appreciate* and *revere* the blood of Jesus, perhaps in greater measure than any other generation. To make it our 'testimony' is to wield the knowledge of the blood in our speech, our worship, our prayer, our conversation. We will increasingly frame our lives and expectations by it. The understanding, grace and internal strength this produces will lead us to willingly forfeit our own lives if necessary in the same spirit of the radical mercy and sacrifice of Christ Himself.

We will overcome resistance, oppression and persecution by the blood. We will live undiluted lives. We will conquer, which is to say the world will not have the final say, but as purified and surrendered vessels, we will finish our course with strength.

Through it all, we will testify of the Lamb. More, not less.

At the end of the age, this is how **"the *salvation* and *power* and *kingdom*…of Christ (will) come."**

How do you spell revival? Salvation. Power. Kingdom come. That's how Revelation 12:10 spells it.

And the key is the blood of the Lamb.

Misspelling Revival

Like so much of our walk with God and so much of church history, our view of revival no doubt needs re-centering, recalibration. Without knowing or realizing it, some wrong views have crept in. God patiently permitted Covid to reveal our mixture, our faulty foundations, our lack of divine wisdom. Revival itself was in danger of becoming an idol by which we could measure our success, rather than being rigidly constrained to the pleasure and glory of God's relentless intention to exalt and celebrate His Son across the earth.

For all these reasons, friends, let me assure you: the coming revival is bigger, not smaller, than what we were looking for. God remains far more serious about a sweeping revival – true global awakening, marked by radical healings, mass salvation and powerful deliverance – than us, but we must accept the chastening to see that true revival will likely also be more holistic, more far-reaching, more eschatological, and more disruptive than what we previously supposed. It will dismantle paradigms, faulty thought systems, and the social, political, and financial infrastructures they support. Revival won't be about your church service, or your success metrics. It will be about the full formation and expression of Christ in your person, and in your midst. It won't be about programs but prayer, power and proclamation.

Anywhere, everywhere.

More than anything, at its core, revival will be a celebration and reenactment of the triumph of Christ. Our message will be Christ and Him crucified. We will have one word, one prophecy, one victory in which to boast: the blood of the Lamb.

His sacrifice. The cross. The precious blood He spilled. It all means something. It means deep and glorious things. It means God's agenda pushes history, not the other way around. His blood carries power. His cross is a mystery, the only path to resurrection. There is no poured out Spirit without poured out blood.

Can we again become fascinated, awestruck, and enraptured with gratitude, by the precious gift of Christ's blood? In this book, we will look at blood, Communion, Passover and the promise of planet-shaking revival (though it may look different than we think). We are going to review current, key dreams and ancient, hopeful prophecies. We are going to briefly investigate key types and shadows found from the garden to Golgotha, from Leviticus to the Lord's Prayer, weaving a tale of many strands, from a blood-soaked road to the broken body of a bleeding Savior. Since Communion distills the primary transaction by which the new covenant is realized, we must take time to understand how the new is drastically superior to the old, or we will miss the point.

The progression of *The Great Communion Revival* operates within a definite thematic narrative, but is really a series of impressionistic vignettes. I am stubbornly determined to keep the book brief but meaty, where each chapter can provide filling, savory appetizers more than a complete meal. Yet by the end, I trust your spirit will feel quite full.

My goal is fourfold:

1. Mine the rich typologies of Scripture to provide vision, language and faith to help us better appreciate and appropriate the power of the blood of Jesus in our lives, families and communities

2. Radically orient us toward the superior work of Christ above Law to raise up sons and daughters who will commune confidently with Him in humility and love

3. Convey current divine intelligence revealed through dreams and the present promptings of the Lord to better discern what is most on His heart for the 2020s

4. To nudge your curious exploration of the Word on these matters, and to help you begin experimenting with a more vibrant expectation of the experience of Communion

I know one thing for sure. Whatever shakings the Father might deem necessary to position His Son at the center of all affections, glory and honor...*that* will be revival.

NOTES & REFLECTIONS

chapter 2

JUDGING THE POWERS

*"...on ALL THE GODS of Egypt
I will EXECUTE JUDGMENTS."*

Exodus 12:12

The Great Communion Revival

Considering the global plague that struck the earth in 2020, is it any coincidence that our Communion dreams would resume in earnest that same year? ***When there is a plague in the land, the people of God should look for the pass over.*** In one of the first given to us that year, another dreamer heard a declaration in his dream: "All the revivals that have ever been in history will dull compared to the Great Communion Revival."

Note: the Blood Communion Revival was now being called the Great Communion Revival. *(I will synonymously employ both phrases in this book).* Note also how in the day of deliverance the blood becomes prominent again. It becomes a sign among the people.

It was so in our dreams. Flood gates opened, as God began to give dream after dream. In still another 2020 dream, the earth was beginning to vibrate with a particular sound.

> "In the dream, Lou instructed others to 'get down and listen' (pointing again to our need to be humble and attentive to the prophetic word of the Lord). The dream continued as people put their ear to the ground.
>
> Someone said, 'I hear cleansing, I hear forgiveness.'
>
> Lou said, 'Yes, but listen again.'
>
> Then a voice declared, "Decree unto the pharaohs of this land: 'My sons, you are My sons, you are My firstborn, you are My princes. The Great Communion Revival can't be stopped.' Wherever the blood is honored the cities will become sheep cities. Where it is dishonored will become goat cities or countries. The only reversal is the honoring of the blood.'"

Honoring the Blood

More than anything else, that is the aim of this book: to *honor the blood of Jesus*.

Blood embroiders all of Scripture together with a bright, scarlet thread of redemption. It begins in Genesis and continues through Revelation. Of particular note, as I share different dreams, note how succinctly they highlight the same biblical themes we will explore. For example, the voice in the dream above declared, "Decree unto the pharaohs of this land: 'My sons, you are My *sons*, you are My *firstborn*, you are *My princes*. The Great Communion Revival can't be stopped.'"

Consider pharaoh, the target of the warning in this dream. Pharaoh was the ruler of ancient Egypt, but he was more than just a king. Pharaoh represented the dark, symbiotic union between the gods of Egypt and their human throne puppet. Regarded as the son of Amun-Ra, pharaoh directly represented the god's will and power on earth. The "pharaohs of the land" thus represent spiritual powers oppressing the people of God through the conspiratorial agency of human powers. In other words, it wasn't just a man who held Israel in bondage, nor just the governmental system represented by his throne, but demonic powers working together with the man and his throne.

To which God had an answer: His Word to these dark powers ('Decree unto the pharaohs!') is actually intended for the hearing of His people ('*My* sons...'") to produce a new and deeper understanding of our relationship ('You are My *sons*'), our stature ('My *firstborn*'), and our authority ('My *princes*') all by virtue of our relation to the God of Israel. In other words, God is stirring Himself to challenge pharaoh once more, which means another

Exodus is coming. God will once again judge the gods of Egypt, even *all* the gods. Though Christ has triumphed on the cross, nations remain under territorial powers until they are displaced by the power of the gospel.

How will they be freed?

> **though Christ has triumphed on the cross, nations remain under territorial powers until they are displaced by the power of the gospel**

A Conspiracy of Kings

The sort of deviant, malevolent tactics by which rebel spirits and lawless humans have shaped the general arc of history increasingly seems to control the headlines of the 2020s. Stated differently, a conspiracy of kings is heavily at work in the halls of power. Under the anointing of the Holy Spirit, in Psalm 2, King David pulls back the curtain on those shadowy meetings to reveal the cause of secret things running amok in the world – things truly dark and corrupt, yet often hidden to the casual observer. The pharaohs of the land have an agenda.

> **"Why are the *nations in an uproar*, and the peoples devising a vain thing?** *The kings of the earth take their stand*, **and the *rulers take counsel together* against the LORD and against His Anointed."** (Psalm 2:1-2)

What is their mission statement? Their common goal?

"Let's get free of God!" (Psalm 2:2, MSG)

When rulers privately take counsel together to plot a unified rebellion, that's called a conspiracy. It's not just a theory. Knowingly or unknowingly (and likely both), a dark cabal of powerful humans and malicious, invisible powers are coordinating their rebellion against God to manifest "on earth as in heaven." This conspiracy is prophesied to accelerate and mature at the end of the age. My point: there is a reality *behind* the reality to which humans are privy.

God's answer in Psalm 2 is to install His own chosen King on Mount Zion. Christ, the anointed, eschatological ruler of history, will judge and ultimately overthrow the corrupt, conspiratorial "kings" (on earth and in heaven) through dynamic intercession by which He will inherit the earth (i.e. God tells Him, **"*Ask* of Me, and I will surely give the nations as Your inheritance"** v. 8, NASB).

This judgment of the powers has been partially realized in the present but will be fully achieved in the inheritance of nations, a Messianic promise similarly described in Psalm 82.

> **"God has taken His place in the divine council;**
> *in the midst of the gods He holds judgment*:
> **'How long will you judge unjustly**
> **and show partiality to the wicked?' Selah**
> **'Give justice to the weak and the fatherless;**
> **maintain the right of the afflicted and the destitute.**

> **Rescue the weak and the needy;**
> **deliver them from the hand of the wicked.'**
> **They have neither knowledge nor understanding,**
> **they walk about in darkness;**
> **all the foundations of the earth are shaken.**
> **I said, 'You are gods,**
> **sons of the Most High, all of you;**
> *nevertheless, like men you shall die,*
> *and fall like any prince.'*
> **Arise, O God, judge the earth;**
> **for** *you shall inherit all the nations!*" (Psalm 82)

In other words, part of the greatest revival in history will inevitably involve the greatest challenge to iniquitous powers in history. The only comparable period to comprehend the drama and scale of the coming upheaval, including signs, wonders and geopolitical turmoil is the original exodus from Egypt. According to Micah 7:15-16, that past clash of God against gods serves as a model for future, miraculous deliverance – "marvelous things" – on a scale never before seen on the earth.

Challenging Pharaoh

"Decree unto the pharaohs of this land: 'My sons, you are My *sons*, you are My *firstborn*, you are *My princes*. The Great Communion Revival can't be stopped.'"

Are you starting to see more in this simple, piercing dream? I can almost imagine it was given in "2020" because the Lord wanted to begin fitting us with new lenses to better focus His people on the astonishing ways He will manifest His glory in the days ahead. So if the mafioso of human and demonic powers holding the world in bondage (as symbolized by pharaoh) has been scheduled for a power-breaking confrontation, what is it?

Tell pharaoh: "The Great Communion Revival *can't be stopped!*"

No doubt, there will be resistance. Pharaoh partially represents the pride and presumption that refuses to yield to Yahweh's command: "Let My people go!"

God told Moses, "Go tell pharaoh…"

God is doing the same thing in the dream: "Tell the pharaohs of the land."

I believe this signals an unprecedented clash of kingdoms coming to the earth in the days ahead, with *the core of the challenge being centered upon acts of Communion, i.e. how deeply we are meant to experience God's protection, fellowship and empowerment through the atoning power of Jesus' blood.* Correspondingly, we *tell*, declaring His triumph to every high place, every principality and power.

Countless Bible prophesies attest to troubles coming, but as with the passage in Micah, the dream is nudging us to look back to the Exodus if we wish to look forward to what God will do next, and how. Part of the lesson is that power alone was not the cause of deliverance. How was Israel finally rescued from Egypt? Yes, the gods of Egypt were judged (Numbers 33:3-4), but the rescue was a *ransom*. A blood price was paid. An exchange was made. Nine plagues properly humiliated the gods of Egypt, but it was the tenth that broke the back of pharaoh's power and pride. The same tenth plague that left the firstborns of Egypt dead in the streets left the firstborns of Israel alive in their homes.

Arbitrarily spared by God? No, *passed over.*

In both cases, Egypt's and Israel's, the blood of the firstborns was required, but in Israel's case a substitution was made for their salvation. Any Jewish son that was not found in a home marked by blood when the destroying angel passed by would have perished along with the sons of Egypt.

The difference – the *only* difference – was lamb's blood.

Those who experienced judgment and death versus those who experienced mercy and life were distinguished by a single characteristic – not genetics or ethnicity, not socioeconomic status, nor meritorious deeds. It did not matter whether you were the son of a slave, priest, or king. No, the only question was whether your home was stained with blood. What is a home? It is where you live, feed, fellowship and take shelter from the storm. Do you "live" marked by an innocence that is not your own? By this fact alone, God identified those who were His people, and those who were not. Those in the family of God, under His protection and mercy, are those under the blood. *Zero* exceptions.

To this day, Jews still celebrate the Passover every Spring as one of three annual High Holy Feasts, and the most defining moment in Jewish history. In fact, God commanded that the new nation restart their calendar. Each new year would begin with Passover (Exodus 12:2). That's how momentous this moment was, this night of innocent blood. It restarted history.

For thousands of years, according to talmudic tradition, Jewish children have been trained to ask, "Why is this night special from all other nights?" This question sets up a recitation of the events of the Exodus and adds meaning to every stage of the Seder meal. Israel exists as a nation today because of a celestial rescue plan where thousands of innocent lambs were slain all over ancient Egypt in the territory of Goshen so that blood could be wiped across the doorposts and lintels of their homes.

The blood was a sign. It declared: this house is ransomed, the price is paid. At the sight of the blood, the angel of death would pass over each Israelite home, but the Egyptian home next door or across the street not so marked were not passed over. Again, Israel was not *ignored.* The firstborn sons of Israel did not merely survive by neglect; no, they were purchased, exchanged. The lamb was slain in place, in proxy, for the death sentence they carried.

Thousands of years later, another Son, the only begotten, firstborn of God would be similarly afflicted by the curse of death, not of His own doing, but for the deliverance of a people. Not just some people, but all people. In the same breath, He would also become the innocent lamb whose blood was shed that God's wrath might pass over. With the single sacrifice of His own life, in the most mysterious convergence of every mythic type prophesied for the Savior of the World, Jesus became the guilt we could not bear, took the curse we could not survive, and shed the blood that granted mercy and life.

Birth and Deliverance

To commemorate His historic accomplishment – that great mystery for which prophets longed and history awaited – the Lord instituted something. Ever after that night, His disciples were to obey a simple command. An act of remembrance:

Communion.

The Christian sacrament of Communion is a new covenant reenactment of the historic deliverance of Passover night, remembered by the Lord and celebrated with His disciples on Passover night (Luke 22:8, 15). Many don't realize that there is no Communion ritual without Passover remembrance. The very same night that Jesus was betrayed and sentenced to die is the very night that children all over Israel were asking their fathers, "What makes this night different from every other?"

Centuries after the first Passover, the prophet Ezekiel reimagined that day as a birthing event.

> **"And as for your birth,** *on the day you were born* **your cord was not cut, nor were you washed with water to cleanse you . . .** *When I passed by you and saw you wallowing in your blood, I said to you in your blood, 'Live!'* **I said to you in your blood, 'Live!'"** (Ezekiel 16:4-6)

Ezekiel poetically recognized that the Passover operated on at least two levels. At a personal level, the blood of the lamb saved (granting life), but at a national level, the same blood *delivered* (something was born). Literally, like a birth canal releasing blood so that the baby can come forth, Israel was emancipated from bondage to freedom, from death to life.

In the clash of cosmic empires that is coming, sheep nations and goat nations will partially be determined by whether their culture honors and defends the *imago dei*, the sanctity of life, the value and meaning of bloodlines (marriage, family, gender), and therefore the merciful gift of salvation by which Christ restores humanity's original design and destiny. The fact that the uncreated Son of God *chose* to become a Son of Man is to say He needed blood so that He could bleed, which is to say that men and women are designed in God's image in such a manner that *blood means something very important.* Even the fringes of this thought begs for a radical reappreciation of the wonder and sacred dignity of human life.

While personal aspects of redemption manifest at the individual level, they coagulate into culture-shaping influence. Nevertheless, the blood of Jesus will not be limited to social metrics and sociological reform. Communion will also become a weapon of spiritual proportion, reenacting the judgment and triumph of Christ over all other gods. How this will play out remains to be seen.

Also, if the word 'judgment' scares you (as it does many Christians), we need to recalibrate. Most people tend to think of judgment in only negative terms, but the value of any judgment is entirely dependent on who is judging and why. The righteous judgment of Yahweh on the gods of Egypt was *good* for the sons of Israel. Jacob's family had entered Egypt, like a seed in a womb, but a nation would emerge. Ezekiel recognized this: how could the baby nation come out otherwise, but with blood? Such is salvation. Such is birth.

It is no coincidence that the birthing process is also referred to in terms of deliverance. When a baby is born, it is because the mother goes into labor, and the doctor or midwife helps to deliver.

What we call the Last Supper is actually Jesus celebrating Passover with his closest friends before going to the cross to become the Passover lamb of God. He went to the cross to save each of us at a personal level, but also to birth, or deliver, the new humanity that would comprise the nation of God. He took the fate of slaves and, with His own blood, said, "Live!"

The wages of Adam's sin, having infected humanity with far more devastating consequence than any pandemic, were now marked for termination *in the dwelling*, the incarnate body, of the Firstborn of God. To join with Christ by faith is to enter into the habitation of heaven, Christ's body, where God dwells. Even as Israel entered their own blood-marked homes, Jesus' broken body becomes our "safe house," eternally marked with blood.

There, inside Christ, we are safe from the storm. We are not merely granted life; to be born again with eternal blood is to receive an eternal destiny. From whipping stripes, we are healed, and from the wounded place of His side, where blood and water spilled, Christ has caused a holy kingdom of royal priests to arise.

Part of the question of this book is to ask: how *can we stay in* Christ? What pulls us in and out of His presence? How can we hide in His shadow, in a dwelling marked with blood?

Reenacting the Triumph of the Cross

Communion (some use the latin term, 'Eucharist') is part of the answer. History shifted when the Lamb was slain. Communion is the ongoing remembrance of that colossal, staggering event. When His blood spilled, a new redemptive calendar began. The Kingdom age of mercy and triumph over the law of sin, death, accusation and condemnation.

The Apostle Paul said,

> **"For as often as you eat this bread and drink the cup, you *proclaim* the Lord's death until He comes."** (1 Corinthians 11:26)

What does it mean to proclaim the Lord's death?

First, notice the eschatological tenor of the act. The church is to do this thing *until* the Lord returns. According to Paul, therefore, Communion is not just eating bread and drinking juice. Paul's language suggests that the act itself is some sort of wild proclamation of victory that is meant to nourish and sustain us. When we eat and drink, we prophecy a continuity between His first and second coming, between the eternal triumph of His cross and the total triumph of His glorious return.

The reenactment and fulfillment of Passover on the cross at the cosmic level is not the kind of event one should treat casually, yet by and large, Protestants have been guilty of just that. In our zeal to correct what we perceived as the heresies and idolatries of medieval Roman Catholicism, we stripped Communion bare, turning it from a mystery to a liturgy, from liturgy to memento; from a feast of the real presence of Christ to an occasional corporate duty scheduled regularly for Sunday church.

Thankfully, this is changing, but I believe we've barely scratched the surface. What is yet to come will truly be dramatic, and it will come from many directions, many traditions, many teachers, and from many familiar Bible passages we will begin to see in a whole new light. The Lord is going to follow His own dictum. As master of His house, He will **"bring out of his treasure what is new and what is old"** (Matt. 13:52).

Practically, this means we can discover things we've never before seen in the Word (new treasures) or can be freshly moved to obey or utilize things we once knew, but have grown dim or dull within us (old treasures).

> **in our zeal to correct what we perceived as heresies, we stripped Communion bare, turning it from a mystery to a liturgy, from liturgy to memento; from a feast of the real presence of Christ to an occasional corporate duty scheduled regularly for Sunday church**

We know, and perhaps take for granted, that Scripture is strewn with countless deep riches, but I want to dig deeper still and rediscover some of those "veins." Veins of truth, yes, but the pun is obvious. We need an arterial transplant, a beating heart, and a fresh infusion of blood theology. I want to see what I've missed, and believe what I've seen. The narrative of Scripture is soaked with blood. It's in plain sight, but also hidden. We need it all.

We have lost too much of the power of His blood and are spiritually anemic as a result. The only way to become strong in the blood again is to recover the humbling awe and majestic triumph of Christ, the Lamb of God.

EXCURSUS A

"A Brief Theology for Spiritual Warfare"

Paul understood the events of the Old Testament as profoundly applicable, relevant tutorials for new covenant believers. **"These things happened to them as an example, but they were written down for our instruction, on whom the end of the ages has come"** (1 Cor. 10:11). In other words, we are meant to recognize and apply the patterns of the Old Testament as thematically repeatable events even unto the *eschaton*, the final moments of the theater of history.

Secondly, these symbols operate on multiple levels. Pharaoh was a real historical figure, but he can also represent the general problem of evil human power, or an enslavement system (as he did for African Americans), or he can represent Satan and Egypt as a type of the bondage of sin and death from which Christ (typified by Moses, the Deliverer) rescues us. While the history is fixed, the symbols are malleable props in the hands of the Lord.

However, *any spiritual warfare principle that seeks to replicate or re-achieve the victory which Christ single-handedly and eternally accomplished by virtue of His cross and resurrection is a dangerous error.* In His exalted position as King of Kings and Lord of Nations, the victory has already been secured, to which we can add nothing. At the same time, multiple passages, plus clear evidence of systemic, ongoing darkness, not to mention the climactic nature (and requirement) of the Second Coming, should fully convince us that history's total conformity to the will of God has not yet been realized. Thus, it would be consistent with the nature of God to reference previous movements and deliverances recorded in Scripture as evidence or types of divine initiatives by which He will continue to shape history unto that final day of perfect triumph. In this great endeavor, we are not merely participants, but partners.

We should therefore be both bold and cautious in our application. We must not fail to war in the spirit, nor draw upon the typology of Scripture for faith, inspiration and instruction. Equally so, we must not think we are somehow achieving, rather than merely enforcing, what Christ has already accomplished.

---

chapter 3

A DOOR OPENS

"Blessed be the name of God forever and ever, to whom belong wisdom and might. HE CHANGES TIMES AND SEASONS; He removes kings and sets up kings; He gives wisdom to the wise and knowledge to those who have understanding; HE REVEALS DEEP AND HIDDEN THINGS…"

Daniel 2:20-22

L ike jumpstarting a car, more dreams suddenly began popping up in 2020. Obviously, we sensed something was stirring. The Lord was alerting us. After all those years, He was saying, "I want you to start paying attention again." So we did, but we still didn't have the sense of timing. After all, it had been roughly 20 years since the initial dream.

But then, after several more (sprinkled across later chapters), another key dream in 2021 seemed to point in part to the matter of timing. In the dream, the Lord put Israel in the center of the story by showing a headline in a newspaper called, *The Israeli Times*. In this dream, the "sons of Israel" had lost their sense of identity (they couldn't find their wallets and ID cards) when a warning was announced: "We are in a holy war and our fight is not flesh and blood but against a global pandemic."

The dream revealed this particular pandemic was not Covid, but a toxic, anti-semitic spirit spreading rapidly across the earth. Holy war was being declared by heaven to rescue the sons of Israel from the danger of a wrong identity. (Remember, God will often "stack" dreams upon one another, extending a common storyline, confirming themes, and clarifying or expanding the symbolism to get a clearer sense of the mission He wants to impart).

We saw a connection between the dream from the last chapter where God challenged pharaoh by confirming Israel's identity – "you are My *sons*, you are My *firstborn*, you are My *princes*" – and the dream warning about lost IDs. Putting the two together, could it be that a missing link between Israel's lost identity and their true identity is to be found in a deeper revelation of their own Passover story? After all, the answer to the identity crisis was a "Great Communion Revival that could not be stopped!"

Similarly, as Israel can also symbolize the church – we who have become sons of God through faith (Rom. 8:14, Gal. 3:7, 26, 29); the Israel of God (Gal. 6:16); a royal priesthood and holy race (1 Pet. 2:9-10); and a wild vine grafted into the rootstock of promise (Rom. 9:8, 24-26, 11:17-19) – could part of the Great Communion Revival also be to provoke the Gentile church to reexamine the mysteries of blood's atoning power, the kinds of truths upon which the priesthood of Israel was built?

In other words, could a Great Communion Revival be part of uniting Jew and Gentile in the final plan of God? Could Old Testament Passover and New Testament Communion become a shared history that begins to simultaneously remove the veil that lays upon Israel, while deepening the roots of Gentiles who have for centuries treated Communion rather superficially? Doesn't it make sense that a deeper experience of our Communion with Christ would dramatically deepen and strengthen the root system of our identity in Christ?

What might the Lord be doing? What doors are unlocking?

I don't fully know, but I think it's bigger than we can imagine. Years ago, He gave me a dream to help expand my thinking.

Resurrection Life for People and Planet

In the dream I was boldly and emotionally preaching about the promised resurrection of the believer in the Day of the Lord. I wept at the hope and sweetness that death itself would one day be defeated, completely swallowed up in life. Humanity's common grief over lost loved ones would be conquered at last as every believer received their glorified, perfected bodies and countless generations came together to live eternally in the kindness of God. This will only happen when Christ's triumph over the grave finally and equally manifests in our own mortal bodies. I woke at 11:12 pm with tears on my pillow. Upon waking, I was surprised by a strong sense of the Lord's presence, and even more surprised by His internal voice.

He said, *"Romans 11:12 is the end of the Roman Road. My people know where salvation begins, but they don't know where it ends. It ends at Romans 11:12."*

Older believers will recognize that language, but younger ones might not. For decades, the classic "Romans Road To Salvation" has been a simple, effective evangelistic tool to help Christians witness to others. It typically employs four simple verses or "steps" on the road: Romans 3:23, 6:23, 5:8 and 10:9. Each of these progresses further, so that an unbeliever can recognize their sinful state, then move toward salvation in Christ.

However, in my dream, the Lord challenged the view that salvation was strictly personal. There are degrees of finality beyond the personal, a dimension by which the grip of sin and death on the whole planet will one day be broken. In pointing to that period of time, Paul posed a thought experiment in Romans 12. If glorious riches of salvation were released to the nations in the Jew's rejection of Christ and their subsequent blindness, how much more amazing will be the power and grace released by their eventual *acceptance* of Messiah? Paul poses the question in verse 12, gives the answer, and then expands the answer in verse 15: it will be nothing less than "life from the dead."

Literally, resurrection life.

> **"Now if their trespass means riches for the world, and if their failure means riches for the Gentiles,** *how much more will their full inclusion mean!*...**For if their rejection means the reconciliation of the world, what will their acceptance mean but** *life from the dead?*" (Romans 11:12,15)

Life from the dead for an entire planet? How difficult, but glorious to imagine! Surely we can all see *revival* in those words (literally)! So if Israel's salvation lies in part in their provocation to jealousy by Gentiles who walk in fellowship with *their* God (Romans 10:19, 11:11), I must ask again: could a Great Communion Revival be part of uniting the family of God through a profound resurgence of the ultimate Passover story?

Many will dismiss these open-ended questions as too speculative, but our entire community has lived for years in the simple belief that God delights in revealing secrets that invite us into deeper intercession. So when the "Lost ID / Israeli Times" dream ended with the dreamer seeing multiple twenty dollar bills scattered all over the floor, in dream fashion he *knew* that all the "20s" spoke to the 2020s (with the strange math of the dream "all adding up to 2022"). In simple faith, we began to set our gaze toward something beginning in 2022.

For those who are new to the unique flow of revelation that can happen between the Word and the Spirit, and the mysterious world of dreams, it's difficult to fully capture the dynamic manner in which the Holy Spirit breathes upon the kind of corporate moments of revelation I'm describing, but it can be explosive. Not just with emotion, but with clarity, conviction and faith.

Something bears witness, then another word confirms it, several other passages of Scripture come alive in that unique context, and a gift of faith is born. There is a pristine quality to these moments that our team has learned to cherish and watch for. We've cultivated a "present" watchfulness, ready and alert for the Lord's voice. Sometimes we get it wrong, but sometimes we get it right.

"Next Year in Israel!"

After more prayer and pondering, we began to believe that the Lord was perhaps pointing to 2022 as *the beginning* of the beginning of the Great Communion Revival. During this same period, a few other data points also became clear, confirmed in the Word, and highlighted with urgency in our dreams:

- Pray for the salvation of Israel, i.e. **"To the Jew first!"** (Rom. 1:16). Israel is central to the Lord's covenantal dealings with all humans. Eschatology cannot be understood apart from that fact

- Go to Jerusalem and take Communion on Good Friday (Passover) with other leaders (a couple of dreams had alerted us to this journey perhaps happening suddenly)

- Begin taking Communion in a more meaningful way and with greater frequency

- Begin publicly articulating the small bits of revelation we had, and ask the Lord for more

In 2021, we began longing and asking the Lord if we could take Communion in Israel in 2022. "Next year in Israel," we said, echoing the sentiments of Jews who seek to take Aliyah to the

Holy Land. There had been enough indicators at that point that we felt our next step was to simply "do the dreams." (Lou has carefully taught and demonstrated this principle over many years). But there was a problem: Israel was among the most tightly restricted Covid nations. It was locked down.

In early 2022, a handful of us undertook a 21-day fast at a little house of prayer called "The Door" at the foot of Pike's Peak. What made it even more interesting, or painfully ironic, was that the Hebrew and Gregorian calendars lined up in 2022 for Passover and Good Friday to land on the same day, something that has only occurred 34 times in the last 100 years (but with greater frequency so far this century).

But what could we do? The "door" to Israel was closed. We resigned ourselves to doing a Zoom livestream with others in Jerusalem, which hardly felt the same. Then, totally unexpectedly, on February 22 (2-22-22) Israel announced that it would open it's borders beginning March 1 of that year.

"...**He shall open, and none shall shut**" (Isaiah 22:22).

Suddenly, the door was open. We bought our tickets and headed east. On April 15, 2022, Lou and I and several other leaders from various nations gathered in the historic building of Christ Church, the first Protestant church in the Levant, located just 200 yards from the Jaffa Gate in the Old City. Founded in 1842 by a German-born Jew named Michael Solomon, who began his work as the first Anglican Bishop in the Holy Land, Christ Church was pastored (at the time) by two Messianic Jewish brothers, Reuven and Benjamin Berger. In other words, the setting seemed beautifully appropriate for a reverent, hopeful act of Jews and Gentiles remembering and celebrating the Passover sacrifice of Christ.

We streamed it online, called it a Global Communion. It was small. We chose to rejoice in small beginnings. If something added up to 2022, we would rather swing and miss than not swing at all.

Out of these small efforts, we began to hear that others were also having "Communion dreams." Even more amazing, it soon became clear that God was doing something well beyond the world of dreams. We began to hear of believers in other cities and nations who were not only dreaming, but feeling nudged by the Lord to begin practicing Communion in a new way. In some instances, we received reports that people had already been doing this for many years under the prompting of the Holy Spirit.

we began to hear of believers in other cities and nations who were feeling nudged by the Lord to begin practicing Communion in a new way

These believers were taking daily Communion – daily bread and wine in their home – but not as a formality or ritual to complete. It was becoming something more to them. True food. A spiritual feast. A Sacrament of grace bringing fresh revelation and encounter with God. They had thought they were alone because no one else was talking about it, but as Lou and I began to give voice to this idea of a Blood Communion Revival in various places where we spoke, including online, reports came flooding in.

Perhaps something small, but important, was adding up in 2022.

SECTION TAKEAWAYS

1. God's will is a reflection of His purpose, intentions and desires. For God to desire something out of the mysterious, inscrutable depths of His infinite Being helps to explain the highly symbolic mechanism by which humans also dream. Since Eden, God's "dream" has been for full fellowship with humanity and also the glorification of His Son.

2. A divine dream now manifesting in the earth relates to God's intention to increase the church's understanding of Communion as a key to knowing and experiencing Jesus more deeply.

3. The Great Blood Communion Revival points to a new convergence of the Passover motif as God delivers His people, marks us with His blood, and judges the gods of the world.

NOTES & REFLECTIONS

BETTER THINGS

chapter 4

A TEMPLATE FOR BETTER REVIVAL

"Though commended through their faith...GOD HAD PROVIDED SOMETHING BETTER FOR US"

- Hebrews 11:39-40

If a great revival is coming that will replicate the cosmic implications of what the Exodus and Passover meant for the Jews, albeit at a global level, then surely we stand on the cusp of one of the few, true hinge points of human history.

This should give us pause. You may have heard that insanity is doing the same thing over and over while expecting different results. Since every previous revival inevitably declined into irrelevance, what do we need to get right that other generations have gotten wrong? In the late 1950s, Leonard Ravenhill wrote *Why Revival Tarries*. We know what ingredients tend to trigger revival: relentless prayer, personal humility, unction, prophetic fire, deep longing for God.

I'm asking, why does revival end?

While human zeal can reflect divine desire and produce temporary, impressive, perhaps even semi-divine results, such zeal eventually comes at a cost when it subtly shifts from the power of God to the passion of the person. Historically, nearly every previous revival has eventually degraded into human striving, boasting or self-righteousness. This poses a quandary for sustaining revival because God is 100% committed to resisting pride.

Connect the dots and we can see how genuine revival *could eventually become resisted by God Himself.*

An unfortunate cycle ensues: should a revival seem to ebb, the minister and people will strive harder. Subtly, we become the center of the revival story, so God resists more and more. In turn, the people strive more and more, so zealous for the feeling of revival that we will have it *with or without God.* What legitimately may have begun as a work of the Holy Spirit devolves into a work of the flesh. More to the point, *a work of performance more than grace.*

I cannot help but wonder if these "Communion dreams" are meant to interrupt our assumptions of what makes for revival and fine tune our pursuit of it. How do we keep from veering back toward the addition of certain theological errors or human manipulations that are mostly considered "how revival gets done" unless He interrupts our thinking with a new (or at least, purer) idea? *Nothing so completely destroys our self-righteousness more than a true encounter with the broken body and precious blood of Christ.*

What if Communion became heaven's strategy to anchor a future revival not only in Exodus-level magnitude, but in enduring humility, rather than human striving? Could a mighty wave sweep believers into belief again, and lovers into Communion, and followers into friendship? Could the blood of Christ become our greatest hymn, our most important meal, our highest acclaim?

Our natural blood is mostly red, but is also comprised of white cells, the fighter cells. Red cells carry oxygen, nutrients and life. White cells carry infection-fighting power and DNA. In most people who receive a transfusion, it is actually possible to detect trace amounts of the donor's DNA in the recipient's blood for a few days following the procedure. What if we got a blood transfusion by revelation? What forgotten secrets could flow to the Body, unlocking our identity as sons and daughters of God? I daresay new fruit will soon blossom from our sturdy Protestant tree if we humbly correct our Reformation overcorrections and instead learn to bathe our fellowships in the deep memory and sacramental power of the Eucharist once more.

Mass dreams hold potential to become mass movement. Should waves of believers learn to personally and more dynamically appropriate the blood of the Lamb, what might spring forth?

Leveraging Old Things to Understand New Things

One reason we should study the history of the old covenant is to gain enough context to better recognize the total superiority of the new covenant. In this chapter I will briefly explore how the old covenant riches stored in the book of Leviticus point to Christ. But first, Leviticus is not a standalone document. It exists in relation to a bigger story. One of the puzzles Leviticus was designed to answer was this: How can God and man dwell together? The basic scenario involves a true conundrum, both on the human side, and the divine.

How do you survive God?

Of course, God is life and without Him we die, but I'm approaching this from a slightly different angle. Imagine stashing an armed thermonuclear bomb in a canvas tent in the middle of a chaotic refugee camp occupied by 3 million people, any one of whom could wander into the tent and accidentally detonate it? This is not far from the dangerous scenario created by God's loving commitment to dwell among His people.

Though God's tangible presence in the midst of His people was the absolute best thing for them, lit was not without danger to the people He loved. How do we reconcile the irony? What happened? From the very beginning, Scripture emphatically shows how God *always* wanted to dwell among humans. This was the purpose of Creation. God called it good! The Garden of Eden was a designed environment. It was neither an aberration, nor a tease. It was supposed to be normal.

I say again: walking with God, fellowshipping with Him, was intended *by God* as "normal human life."

Tragically, sin made a mess of that from the very start.

walking with God, fellowshipping with Him, was intended by God as "normal human life"

But God didn't quit. He faithfully continued working generally and universally with all humans for a time until two back-to-back incidents, the Great Flood and the Tower of Babel, proved that all humans generally preferred rebellion to obedience.

So God changed tactics. He narrowed His plan to one family.

How did He pick that family? By the evidence of faith.

When a man named Abram from the Chaldean region of Ur responded positively to Yahweh's simple invitation to trust, follow and fellowship together, acting solely by faith, God instituted a covenant of grace and blessing that would extend from Abraham to all his descendants forever.

Mind you, this covenant contained no curse for Abraham, only for Abraham's enemies. All nations would *eventually* be blessed through this covenant, but an important historical footnote is that the Jew-Gentile divide began here.

This is an important detail because for thousands of years to come God would narrow His direct involvement, His purpose, His focus, and His self-revelation, to Abraham's family alone. The legacy of this is secondarily seen in the matchless gift of divinely inspired oracles first entrusted to Jewish prophets, historians and writers. Only through the infallible Word of God can we know God on His own terms, free of the sort of dangerous, manmade contaminations that infect every other religious system. Those truths were entirely entrusted to Abraham's extended family.

However, the primary gift of Abraham's line is *Jesus* Himself. The Messiah, the desire of all nations (Haggai 2:7), is a Jew. The long prophesied answer of God to the problem of sin came from Abraham's seed and none other.

That's not to say the road of redemption was smooth and straight. Rather, it was quite bumpy and convoluted at times. Though God sovereignly utilized even the worst parts, the plot would twist and turn many, many times before His true plan could finally be fully revealed *and* fully understood. In fact, to this day many Christians still do not understand the real point of the story. Here's part of the warning of history we often miss:

Abraham's family did *not* stay in Abraham's *faith*, with vast and negative consequences.

After the deliverance from Egypt, Israel moved from understandable levels of doubt and fear to vicious slander of the essential character and goodness of God. So if you are God, what do you do? What do you do when you cut covenant with a family built on faith that, generations later, refuses to believe. The distant children of Abraham witnessed the most dramatic series of events in human history, a supernatural emancipation process designed entirely for their good, their liberation, their prosperity and welfare.

But they would not believe.

As a result, God did not abandon them, but sovereignly decided another course of action was required.

That path was the Law of Moses, which is best understood as a covenant established concurrent, or parallel, to the covenant with Abraham (Galatians 3:17-25). The need for the Law sprang from Israel's refusal to trust God, but here's an important fact: it neither replaced nor extended Abraham's covenant. Law was, stacked on top, but altogether different.

Abrahams's covenant would never end, but because his descendants refused to relate to Yahweh as Abraham had, God brought the entire nation to Sinai to negotiate new terms for their interaction. Instead of faith-based righteousness, the new deal would require performance-based righteousness.

While it did not replace Abraham's covenant, the Law did supersede it for national and ethnic Israel. The effects were dramatic and immediate. From now on, blessings would not be granted on the basis of trust and relationship, but on obedience and deeds, which meant for the first time Abraham's offspring were now subject to curses for their disobedience, rather than loving discipline in the context of ongoing blessings. Under the terms of the Law, God would continue to dwell among them, but now His holy presence had become a dangerous commodity, for the people were continually judged as unholy and unfit.

Mind you, *none of this was because God Himself had changed, but because the terms of His covenant with Israel changed.* (Remember, God revealed Himself to Abraham face-to-face without peril in Genesis 18).[8] Sin was fatal to body and spirit, but right relationship with God had always been possible by faith, even if only in token form until Christ would be revealed.

This is why future appeals to God's mercy would continue to be based on God's enduring commitment to Abraham, not Israel's faithfulness to Law.[9]

In short, the Sinai Pact changed everything. New terms meant new dynamics were in play. Yahweh still desired His nearness to be both normal and life-giving, but the Sinai Pact also made it fatal. Proximity to God was no longer based on faith, but personal righteousness measured under a conditional covenant that first exposed human sin, then cursed it.

Not a good way to live, but an easy way to die.

Revival That Restores Normal

How does this relate to us? One of the greatest, most insidious deficiencies in the church is our tendency to live more in relation to Moses than Christ. We treat the commands of Moses as the high call of Christian discipleship, rather than the entire purpose of Moses being to point us back to fellowship with God in Christ. We mix the terms of the old and new and think the mixture is what God desires because "it's all in the Bible."

But Hebrews is clear: the old covenant has been rendered obsolete (Hebrews 8:13) in terms of our relationship to God. Yes, the canon of Scripture in the Old Testament remains infallible and authoritative for all time. But when Bible teachers subtly or overtly reinforce the mixture of old and new, then label it discipleship, we lose the time and sequence of the revelation God has brought, and make every covenant the same. If they were the same, we wouldn't have needed more than one!

An old covenant mindset often employs righteous sounding phrases like "it's time to get serious about holiness." While we can all agree on that, most of the time what is intended is for people to get serious about Law. In short, we want people to *behave*. We want to feel like people are changing for good – whether it's true or not!

Such an approach might achieve short term gains, but over the long haul it has never worked and never will, as the Old Testament so clearly attests. You can't be a new creation under the old covenant, nor can you make disciples of Jesus by encouraging (or shaming) them to increase their faithfulness to Moses. That's why you can't build a lasting revival upon Moses. Only Christ.

Like leaven, a performance-based paradigm of discipleship infects everything. It's a poor photocopy of the real deal. Dallas Willard called this faulty photocopy "the gospel of sin management."[10] It's like getting stuck at a traffic intersection on a never-ending roundabout. Discipleship by Law puts us on an endless loop of tasks and check-boxes, dos and don'ts. It keeps us constantly in motion, expending tremendous emotional and spiritual energy, yet we're never able to fully merge onto the highway destined for higher life in God.

(For deeper study, get my book, The Total Superiority of the New Covenant, or my video course at deanbriggs.com/courses).

This is why I believe we do not merely need great revival, we need great *communion*, which can only come by realizing all that God has wrought on our behalf. A Great Communion Revival might just be God's antidote to the tendency of every great revival of the past to drift into legalism, striving and works.

That's also why I believe these dreams are truly heaven sent, because every word matters. It will be *Great* (not small; global in reach, massive in repercussions). It will center upon *Communion* (communing with Christ; co-union; we will rediscover aspects of the majesty of Jesus we've forgotten, or perhaps never knew). And it will bring *Revival* (literally, as the word implies, we will "regain consciousness" and "recover our health"; we will "live again" in the abundant measure of fellowship, fruitfulness and power God intended). The promise of a Great Communion Revival is not to have big meetings where many people get saved, but that *what was once normal for humans in the plan of God can be normal again.*

Leviticus gives us the necessary starting point because it offers the most properly concentrated doctrine of blood in all of Scripture. It establishes a baseline. Jesus reinterpreted Israel's most common blood ritual (Passover) by unequivocally defining part of the mission of the cross as wine we were to drink. He called our cup, "**the *new* covenant in *My* blood**" (Luke 22:20).

Friend, the Mosaic covenant is no longer your judge.

Jesus reinterpreted Israel's most common blood ritual (Passover) by unequivocally defining part of the mission of the cross as wine we were to drink

In this, it is important that we recognize that God Himself did not change from merciful and kind to vengeful and dangerous. He did not suddenly become a different, angry, capricious deity. He is the same yesterday, today and forever. No, the *covenant* changed![11] Israel chose a new arrangement with new rules.

Under the new regime, every person existed in an indefinite state of guilt, i.e. "guilty until proven guilty." We cannot believe God to be truly holy and think otherwise. Nevertheless, because God is also *perfectly and unchangeably good,* He simultaneously embedded in the covenant code a source of energy and comfort greater than the death sentence Israel had chosen.

The greater power was His mercy. The catalyst was blood.

Blood for Mercy

Now under the dominion and consequence of the Law, God showed Moses how to achieve mercy by properly wielding blood. Under the right terms, by sacrifice, Moses would then teach Aaron how blood could become a transport vehicle to move mercy from the innocent to the condemned.

> **Moses taught Aaron how blood could become a transport vehicle to move mercy from the innocent to the condemned**

By definition, a perfect Law could never stop condemning sin without itself becoming sinful. Yet precisely because the Law perfectly reflected God's righteousness, it also provided propitiation for the guilty. It did this because, while judgment and mercy are equally true outcomes of God's justice, He prioritizes them differently.

So yes, one is perfect. But the other is better.

If judgment and mercy each have a voice, only one speaks a better word. So what is possibly more powerful than the wrath of God? Such a question suggests antagonism between the virtues of God, which is false, but at a poetic level the answer remains: mercy, fueled by love. And how is mercy realized? Blood.

This puts explosive power in the understanding of covenantal blood. So now the question is, do you want the power of the old and lesser covenant, or the new and better covenant?

A Better Word from Better Blood

We know that Jesus is **"the mediator of a *new* covenant"** whose blood *"speaks a better word* **than the blood of Abel"** (Hebrews 12:24), but why is it better? The blood of Abel rightly identified the sin of murder and demanded justice. It spoke from the ground and what it said was true: blood demands blood.

"The judgments of the LORD are true; they are righteous altogether" (Psalm 19:9, NASB).

Something can be true, but less than optimal. If justice were the end of the story, we would all be dead. If our "word" – our wounded souls, prayers and pain – unceasingly demands justice from God and others for sins committed against us, we are in the wrong conversation. God's preference reveals His character.

"Who is a God like You, *pardoning iniquity,* and *passing over the transgression* **of the remnant of His heritage? He does not retain His anger forever, because** *He delights in mercy.* **He will again have compassion on us, and will subdue our iniquities.** *You will cast all our sins into the depths of the sea."* (Micah 7:18-19 (NKJV))

Final score: "Mercy triumphs over judgment" (James 2:13).

Thus, the priestly role is ultimately a brotherhood of mercy. Leviticus is the book that reveals their code of blood. Perhaps the most dramatic statement in the entire book reveals how blood equals life.

> **"For *the life of the flesh is in the blood*, and I have given it for you on the altar to make atonement for your souls, for it is *the blood that makes atonement by the life* ... For *the life of every creature is its blood: its blood is its life*."** (Leviticus 17:11,14)

The modern medical blood donation industry and the value of blood infusions in life-threatening situations is proof of Leviticus 17's basic truth, yet this statement is so true to life, so self-evident, it's almost overlooked. In my book, *Longhairs Rising*, I ponder how this passage intuitively connects to the rhythms and maturation cycle of the human experience:

> "Pause to consider your own divine construction as proof of the love-drenched, life-giving power of personal sacrifice. If life is in the blood (Lev. 17:11), then it is no accident that the blood of life would be parabolically revealed in our human frame, particularly in the sexual maturation cycle of men and women. The biological fact of a young girl's transition to mature womanhood occurs when her own body confirms its capacity to bear life with an issue of blood.
>
> Lest we miss the message, this operates on a cycle of renewal. Her body bleeds to prepare her womb, it bleeds when she gives her virginity to a man, and blood again comes forth when a baby is born...baptized in love. She makes a sacrifice of blood for the sake of life. Likewise, a man, according to his own function, goes to war fully prepared to bleed and die defending those he

loves. In both cases, men and women, blood is the evidence of courageous love."[12]

Adam's Blood

Let's peer a little closer. because another mystery is about to unfold in the Hebrew word for blood which is *'daam'*. Do you hear it? *Daam* directly connects to 'A*dam*'.

Here's how it works. The vast majority of ancient Hebrew contained in the Bible can be distilled down to a relatively small number of three-consonant root words. These roots contains the essence of the word's meaning, therefore all words that build upon that root are in some sense an extension of that meaning, as well. The wide vocabulary of biblical Hebrew occurs by changing vowels or adding various prefixes and suffixes to the root. Rabbinical insights frequently involve interpretations derived from the nuanced and interesting relationships that form between words of a common root.

As an example, the words red, blood, soil, and Adam are all word plays derived from a common root. Red is *'adom'*. Soil, dust, earth are all translations of *'adamah'*. (Some have suggested that the original color of a more fertile, mineral rich earth was red, and that Adam's skin tone might have been more reddish brown than our various ethnic skin tones currently convey).

The association of blood *('dam')* with the name Adam signifies not only the biological unity of life, but that life is essentially a covenant contracted in blood, and a contract always comes with a price so perhaps we should not be surprised that blood in plural *('da-mim')* is also the word for money, payment, or retribution.

So many facets to ponder.

More extraordinary still is that because Israel was the only nation to contract a covenant in blood, Israel in some sense considered themselves "new Adam." While no single text makes that claim, a chain of thought between several verses and motifs (beyond the scope of this work) could.

At an archetypal level, the story of Adam is the story of Israel writ small, wherein Genesis 1-3 sees in Adam's story a foreshadow of Israel's creation, mission, unfaithfulness and exile. My point is this: not only is a person a covenantal work of blood, but an entire *people* can also become covenantal by blood.[13]

Sacred Blood

Horror novelist, Clive Barker, distastefully yet accurately observed, "Everybody is a book of blood; wherever we're opened, we're red."[14] Though his genre may be distasteful, the statement is as vividly appropriate as the iron-oxidized red fluid he describes. Stained with those same hues, the Tabernacle complex would have fairly screamed a red-hued message for each new sinner to hear: "This could be your blood, but it is not! A provision has been made. Blood for blood!"

The passion of Jesus conveys equal horror. Every punishment inflicted on our Savior during the events surrounding His false trial and eventual crucifixion made Him bleed. He was beaten and bloodied. He was whipped with a barbed Roman scourge specifically created not to stripe the skin, but to flay the flesh. His crown of thorns dug like a dozen daggers into the skin of His skull. They pulled chunks of His beard out of His face. Finally, the nails and the spear.

Cross became altar.

Christ become both Lamb and Priest.

Visceral and painfully poetic, Barker doesn't realize that his words could be used to describe the connection between Leviticus and Jesus. But the connection is more than poetry. It's quite literal.

The Talmud points out that '*adamah*' (earth) can also be etymologically linked to '*adameh*' (I resemble). The resemblance of man therefore points to God. We know this, but by digging deeper, a wondrous new layer emerges regarding man's design as a reductionist embodiment of God.

In this view, if God's eternal purpose forms the mold of man's biological destiny, then a deeply surprising reason may have compelled God to make Adam "like" Himself. Given the topic of this book, is it any surprise the reason would be blood?

Bear with me. In the ancient world, the table of elements for life was comprised of three substances. I don't mean the pagan tetrad of air, fire, water and earth. For the Hebrew mind, life was to be found in breath (Hebrew, '*ruah*'), water, and the blood of living creatures. As a matter of priority, while water sustained life, blood *was* life.

However, in light of Genesis 1:26, **"Let Us make man in Our image,** *after Our likeness* ('adameh')" we are nudged to double back on God's design and see that for man to be fashioned in God's likeness means *humans are made to bleed because something in the heart of God was prepared to bleed as well.*

Born of God and born of woman...*so that God could bleed.*

We *ademeh* Him. We resemble Him. We embody His purpose, not just His personality. Therefore for God to sovereignly and omnisciently know He will eventually offer His blood is to necessitate our mortal coil in such a manner that *our veins could one day bear the life of God Himself*, and from those veins – truly human veins – offer life to all.

The full wordplay would look like this. God's eternal purpose was for *adamah* to *ademeh* Him enough that the *dam* in Adam could be properly exchanged as *da-mim* for Adam's sin, all to the praise and glory of the Lamb!

I don't know about you, but the mysteries of God hidden in this wordplay leaves me reeling. For want of this ageless, mysterious love story, four Living Creatures, 24 Elders, and myriads upon myriads of angels continue to inquire, gasp in awe, fall down in silence, and burst forth in riotous worship. It is too big, too daring, too wildly magnanimous and kind, to ever look at another human and feel hatred, apathy or scorn for their condition, no matter how low or broken.

Like you, they, too, are the *imago dei*, the very image of God. How dare we not love – for God so loved! In fact, Communion can help us turn the tables in our own heart to finally see both saved and unsaved with the tender, reverential affection of blood kin, sons and daughters of the same Father.

"In the beginning, God created" *with blood in mind*, then fashioned man to fit the plan. Your pumping heart's 60,000 miles of blood vessels, finely threading through your body's tissue, nourishing every system with critical nutrients, oxygen, hormones, electrolytes, vitamins, antibodies and more, bears witness to this divine plan. From the Father's heart of love for all His children, to the liquid love flowing through your veins, the intent of the Trinity was always that the Son become a lamb, and the lamb be slain.

Communion is the living memory of that eternal story.

EXCURSUS B

"Edenic Fellowship Restored"

Being fully God, fully man, and knowing intimately the detailed construction of eternity, history, law, priesthood and covenant, Jesus no doubt spoke to His disciples at the Last Supper with far more drama, joy and hope than we typically read into the text. Knowing every nuance of His Father's eternal plan, the superior grace of His new covenant over the old, plus many more secrets and riches stored up in what would become the triumph of His cross, Jesus did not offer obligatory words like a toast at a wedding. Rather, He proclaimed the emotion of a historic feast, namely that Edenic fellowship between man and God was not only about to be restored, but *surpassed*. With this framework and a little bit of imagination, we can read between the lines of Jesus's short statement an expanded paraphrase along these lines:

"My dearest friends, I love you beyond words. Long have I desired to share this meal with you! I need you to understand what is about to happen. I am about to overturn 1000 years of the crushing requirements by which the human race has been held captive to the Law of sin and death. In the garden, Adam and Eve sought knowledge and perfection apart from the Godhead. What folly, when fellowship with My Father is the only true source of Life!

As I am in My Father and My Father is in Me, so too you truly live only in Us. Any other path is false life, which guarantees death. When Adam and Eve chose a lie for life, they passed the same curse *to all their descendants. At Sinai, the perfect Law perfectly exposed their lies. Though the Law is brilliant, perfect and true, it is no different than the Tree of the Knowledge of Good and Evil: it can never be your source. Having chosen to 'obey the commandments and live' (Deut. 30:16) the Law became a relentless prosecutor of every failure. A debt system accumulated. Failure and personal guilt were thus guaranteed. Even with millions of sacrifices performed over the course of endless centuries, the final record shows that every offering afforded credit insufficient to the real debt. History became a ledger of accumulating judgment.*

"But now I am here! Though Adam was faithless, I am faithful. I am about to restart humanity in My image – a new bloodline. I will restore divine breath to humanity's lungs. You will truly live again! What you know about God is going to forever change, and I Am that change. The old way ends tonight. As I lift this cup before you, My Father is elevating My blood as your only hope. No longer will you be judged for what you do or have done. Henceforth, God the Just will be satisfied to look upon Me and pardon you, for I have completely fulfilled the Law on your behalf. Receive My life in place of yours. Cease striving. Under Moses, the former covenant judged you by your works and deeds. In the new covenant, you are judged by Mine, and I did not come to judge the world, but to save it. So receive My work and rest. This poured out cup, this divine exchange, must only be believed to be received. Drink it deeply. Make it part of your innards. Get it inside you. Soon, My own personality and Spirit will be put inside you, as you are born again of blood and water. What begins right here, right now, is the start of a new creation."

chapter 5

PASSOVER DECADE & PROPHETIC ACTIVISM

"In the middle of a crisis, prophecy"

Chuck Pierce, *The Passover Prophecies*[15]

The Great Communion Revival

Having briefly explored a theology for atoning blood out of Leviticus that remains grounded in a New Covenant perspective, let's dive back into the prophetic storyline once more. First, we need to back up a bit. Though the Great Communion Revival has barely begun in one sense, I also believe we're well into this story from God's vantage point.

Upon writing this book, I found it interesting to discover that the major themes I have explored coincide with observations from other leaders, as well. For example, back in 2019, heading into 2020, a number of traditional Jewish rabbis noted the emergence of a Passover theme for the 2020s, especially since Jews in the land of Israel were largely being confined to their homes once more during a time of plague.

In roughly that same period, unknown to our team, author and teacher, Chuck Pierce, was releasing a series of prophetic words that began in September, 2019. Pierce prophesied that the 2020s would be "The Decade of the Passover" and that we should expect each year of this present decade to unfold the message and importance of Passover in increasingly timely ways.

My friend, Messianic Rabbi, Jason Sobel, described the same idea using insights derived from the Hebrew calendar and alphabet (where each letter corresponds to both a numerical value and a pictorial symbol). The idea is that the Gregorian decade of the 2020s translates to the 5780s on the Hebrew calendar. Because *"pey"* is the Hebrew letter corresponding to the number 80, and because the pictograph of the letter portrays an open mouth (by extension, 'breath' or 'voice'), a number of symbolic insights have been gleaned.[16] Of course, you must test these for yourself, but at minimum, I find them interesting!

For example, *Pesach* (the name for Passover in Hebrew), begins with the Hebrew letter 'p' *(pey)*. Passover reveals several notable instances of *pey*. According to the Talmud, God used the Passover to basically punch Pharaoh in his *pey* (mouth) and knock out his tooth, which is why the hard "p" of Pesach became the soft "f" we hear pronounced in Pharaoh. Thus, the deliverance from Egypt is secured by a word beginning with *pey* that judged Egypt and its ruler, whose name becomes a slightly revocalized version of *pey*, and all of this was led by a man (Moses) who received this mission when he turned 80, which is the numerical form of *pey*.

In our modern context, is it any wonder that the Decade of Pey (Hebrew 5780s) has become a battle for the mouth? Wokism is everywhere, threatening dissenters and truth tellers with intimidation, humiliation, deplatforming and worse. Even in free societies, the only "safe" path now requires intellectual suicide and surrender to whatever narrative has become *de rigueur* among academics, celebrities, media figures and lawmakers (transgenderism, Covid, defunding the police, critical race theory, etc). Refuse and you are a hate monger or bigot.

In other words, keep your mouth shut.

Of course, the tenants of oppression and thought control have been building for a while, but subjectively speaking, the coordinated effort to intimidate you and me into total silence seemingly exploded in the 2020s.

Metaphorically, we could say that the pharaohs of the nations have challenged the core freedoms of western civilization. Equally true, in the very year that we were expecting surges of gospel proclamation, government policies dictated isolation or confinement, and everyone was told (or mandated) to literally cover their mouths!

In his book, *The Passover Prophecies,* Pierce wrote,

> "In August, 2019, I spoke these words:
>
> 'What we are entering into is an era, a decade, called 'speaking forth your liberty.' We are going to see so much upheaval coming in the earth realm that you'll just have to hang on for dear life because there will be so many issues rearranged because of the voices that are coming forth. It's what the whole next decade is about, and each year will have a different significance of how we speak.'
>
> The last sentence is so key for us today. This year is 2020, but each of the nine years following will also have a major issue for us to contend for in battle."

He then added, "The divine interruption is on the way!"

If God is causing or permitting something disruptive at a global scale, it is almost certainly because His goals and methods are loftier than our temporal perspective and preference for comfort can conceive. In this regard, my concern for human freedom is not primarily rooted in politics. Though it can manifest by degrees according to differing political constructs – communism is far more restrictive than a democracy overall – even democracies can vary in the degrees of freedom they afford their citizens.

Yet this misses the point that freedom is first a spiritual reality. It's fundamental to our existence. God designed humans to be free so that we can choose to follow and love Him. Remove that freedom by degrees in the imposition or subtle encroachments of dogmas, doctrines and laws, and you bind a human to the earth realm. Strangle our transcendent essence and self-volition, inch by inch, and a broken person (or broken society) might retreat into slavery simply to survive.

On the other hand, they also might light the rope on fire and start a revolution.

Morris Joseph, a Jewish rabbi born in 1848, wrote, "Passover affirms the great truth that liberty is the inalienable right of every human being."[17]

Could it be that the overreaching noose of totalitarianism is setting the stage for a great, voluntary yearning, a Passover cry for the Deliverer to come once more? Is God preparing a new cry for deliverance in the restless souls of countless millions who have felt the rope tightening around their necks?

> "But the Pharaoh that our ancestors pictured, each and every year, for century after century, when Pesah was celebrated, was more than one man: he was for them every tyrant, every cruel and heartless ruler who ever enslaved the men, women and children of his country.
>
> For our forefathers, Pharaoh was the symbol of all those tyrants who ever acted as though they were gods, and whose will had to be obeyed without question, on penalty of torture or death....The first emancipation was thus only a foreshadowing of all the emancipations that were to follow, and which will yet follow in the days to come."[18]

Like I said, interesting!

So if the human pharaoh of the Exodus history (circa 1300 B.C.?) got his tooth knocked out in the judgments of the Passover, and if God is once again warning the Pharaoh's of the land in the 2020s AD, then the New Covenant Passover ceremony we call Communion is likely part of the mechanism by which God is once again challenging these kings, both human and divine.

Prophetic Activism

To explore this idea further, let's look at the biblical practice of what I call, "prophetic activism." Prophetic activism is the enactment of a divine directive, often in a transrational, symbolic manner that is nonetheless central to the delivery of the message. As a result, the action *is* the message in one sense, and therefore inseparable from the result of the message.

It was quite common for Old Testament prophets to employ symbolic actions as part of their prophecies. In the loosest assessment, we might call these "inspired actions," but to the casual, uninformed observer, such gestures and movements would surely seem unconventional, if not outright silly. Nevertheless, regardless of their immediate practical purpose, *the act of obedience in the prophetic display was critical to the strength or intended impact of the prophetic word it accompanied.*

While some might say the actions were intended purely metaphorically, in many instances it is unclear whether the action symbolized the word given, or was part of God's mechanism for effecting it. Consider this small sampling of prophetic activism throughout Scripture. In some of these, you will note that the actions were commanded; in others, the messenger acted symbolically without a specific directive.

- Moses cast a tree into the bitter waters to make them pure (Exodus 15:22–25)
- Joshua performed a series of symbolic actions in the battle of Jericho, including silent marching, trumpets and loud shouting (Joshua 6:1–16), but merely stretched a spear toward the city of Ai (8:18–19)
- Ahijah tore a new garment into twelve pieces (1 Kings 11:29–31)
- Elisha cast salt into a spring to heal its bitter waters (see 2 Kings 2:19–21)
- Isaiah wrote a name upon a scroll, then united with his wife (8:1–4)
- Jeremiah placed stones in a brick kiln (43:8–13)
- Ezekiel ate a scroll on one occasion (Ezekiel 2:8–3:6). On another, the Lord instructed him to shave his beard, cut his hair, then divide the hair into three parts, after which he was to burn a third of his hair with fire, smite another third with a knife, and scatter the final third to the wind (5:2)
- Elisha commanded Joash to shoot arrows of **"victory over Syria"** out the window and then strike the ground with them (2 Kings 13:14–19)
- Zechariah and others participated in a symbolic coronation ceremony (Zechariah 6:9–15)

- Jesus commanded ceremonial vessels be filled with water before they were poured out as wine (John 2:1-8)
- Jesus verbally commanded the healing of blind eyes in one instance (Mark 10:46-52), then rubbed mud on the eyes of another blind man (John 9:1-7). Again, why?

Consider that worship itself is a form of prophetic activism. Because God is worthy, we are commanded and invited to worship Him. This is not an abstraction, though we often treat it as such. For many, worship has become a religious exercise of stoic reserve and mental contemplation, mostly limited to singing.

By contrast, Biblical Hebrew employs seven distinct words for 'worship' or 'praise' which variously mean *shout, kneel, sing* or *raise your hand*. The Hebrew word *'halel'* can mean to boast, rave or be clamorously foolish. Many passages that employ these words also add other actions, such as bowing or clapping. It would seem the assumption of Biblical worship is that we *demonstrate our worship with sincere but directed physical actions* so that our entire being is involved. In other words, to worship God is to make your body a tool that goes beyond words and melodies. Your mouth, arms, hands and legs becomes the physical, volitional demonstrator of the praise you seek to give.

Thus, at its heart, worship itself is prophetic activism. In fact, the very notion of singing or playing music is to say that you cannot merely *think* your way into worship any more than Moses could have *thought* the bitter water into purity, or Joshua could have somehow *willed* Israel into capturing Jericho.

Though many more instances could be given, as a final example, when Isaiah was commanded by the Lord to **"Go, and remove the sackcloth from your body, and take your sandals off your feet,"** Isaiah obeyed, walking **"naked and barefoot"** for three years. He explained that his action was **"for a sign and wonder against Egypt and Ethiopia"** (Isaiah 20:2-3, NKJV). While no doubt embarrassing, Isaiah's nakedness was like a prophetic publicity stunt. The action itself was part of the "sign" that made Israel "wonder."

All these examples beg the question: what would have happened if those actions had not been taken? What victories hinged upon not just the message Isaiah delivered, but his willingness to display the message physically, to reenact it, thereby *demonstrating* the power, purpose and origin of the word of the Lord? Was there ever a case in Scripture where wise, enlightened disobedience brought about a better result than foolish, simple, obedient faith?

Let's get personal. Let's bring this question to our time. To this very day, what disappointments secretly result from our our unwillingness to act with vigor upon a corpus of enduring revelation that comes from our Lord Himself.

Jesus said: "Do this thing." He said, "Take the bread. Drink the wine. Remember."

Paul said, **"As often as you do, you proclaim."**

In the most hopeful sense, there exists a potential point of unity here among the various theological stances regarding the eucharist. Whether you believe it is purely symbolic, or more than symbolic, I do not think any of us can get around the dynamic, interactive nature of Communion as prophetic activism. Eating bread and drinking wine as Jesus commanded remains a transrational act of obedience, worship, declaration and fellowship with Christ that carries consequence in the spirit far beyond the symbolism.

Can we strengthen this consequence with faith? Can we water it down with tokenism?

> **eating bread and drinking wine as Jesus commanded is a transrational act of obedience, worship, and declaration that carries consequence in the spirit far beyond the symbolism**

What happens when we take Communion half-heartedly, with only minimal understanding or concern? It is highly unlikely that the invisible realms are passive observers. Natural kings may not take note of our participation, but spiritual kings (**"principalities and powers"** Ephesians 2:2, 3:10, 6:12; 1 Peter 3:22, Colossians 2:15, Isaiah 24:21) have a long memory. When the ekklesia physically reenact the triumph of Christ with revelation and faith in Communion, we are shooting "arrows of victory" as a reminder that their day of judgment has already come in the Cross, and will soon be consummated in the Day of Wrath at Christ's return.

Because Passover typology is so profoundly fulfilled in Christ, we should begin to regard Communion as a powerful form of spiritual resistance. Communion gives us a means of prophetic activism by which we refuse to be silent. It is a form of perpetual, spiritual defiance against the pressures of the age, bold proclamation in days of pressurized silence and lies, and relentless war against the accuser of the brethren.

David cried out to the Lord,

> "Arise, O LORD! Save me, O my God!…
> ***break the teeth*** **of the wicked"** (Psalm 3:7)

This is the Decade of Pey, the decade of grand reversals. When we feel surrounded and besieged, overwhelmed by hostile forces and antichrist sentiment, we must see that God is secretly setting the stage to break the teeth of the enemy in our lives. He is preparing a Psalm 23 table – the Table of the Lord – in the midst of our enemies. To "break the teeth" is a picture of silencing the authority and power contained in the voice of the enemy to tear you apart, either by accusation or intimidation, or enslavement with lies.

One day soon, our Deliverer is coming! Until then, we must take up every weapon He has already put in our hands.

Knocking out the Tooth

This was dramatically highlighted by a recent dream involving Dutch Sheets. Dutch shared a dream someone sent him. In the dream, a baseball game was being played and the bases were loaded. Dutch asked the dreamer to "hand me my bat." The dreamer then reached for Dutch's bat. Here's what happened:

"I pulled it *from a large wooden Communion box where it had been locked inside.* As I removed it I could see clearly that the bat was inscribed with Ephesians 1:17. I handed it to Dutch, who said to me, 'What direction should I launch the ball?'

I answered Dutch, "Straight for the throat of the pitcher! Remove his voice!"

The pitcher approached the batter's box and as Dutch stepped into it, said to him, "I am here to take you and this weak team out once and for all. You have no hope of making it out of this batter's box in your right mind. This is my season and you will not steal it from me!"

The enemy pitcher's name was 'Zephon.'

Wait, Zephon? That's a specific name with a specific backstory, so let's pause and glance at Exodus 14, where we see the children of Israel pinned against the Red Sea with no way to cross. Egypt's army is bearing down on them in the last and final charge of Pharaoh's wrath. Humiliated by the death of his son and heir, Pharaoh still refuses to surrender. Proud and vengeful, he has brought his entire army to forcibly recapture the freshly delivered Hebrew slaves who have brought such great destruction upon his kingdom.

So…

"The Egyptians pursued them, all Pharaoh's horses and chariots and his horsemen and his army, and overtook them encamped at the sea…*in front of Baal-zephon*…And Moses said to the people, 'Fear not,

stand firm, and see the salvation of the LORD, which he will work for you today. For the Egyptians whom you see today, you shall never see again. The LORD will fight for you, and you have only to be silent…and I will get glory over Pharaoh and all his host, his chariots, and his horsemen.'" (Exodus 14:9-17)

Actually, if you back up a few verses, you will see in verse one that Israel did not accidentally end up in this spot. God had *commanded* them to camp at that very point, Baal-zephon. Yahewh was staging a moment of confrontation by using apparent weakness to achieve His final, total victory.

Israel was trapped against the Red Sea at Zephon…or was God trapping Pharaoh?

Back to the dream with Dutch, the pitcher named Zephon (which we now understand as the place where you feel pinned against the wall with no options and no hope) had thrown two strikes, but in a plot twist, they were actually strikes against him, not Dutch. For the final pitch, Dutch declared,

> "'This is your last pitch but not my last ball! I will deliver the third strike to you and your house!'
>
> Zephon threw the ball, which Dutch hit with a powerful swing. The ball found its mark, a line drive to the throat of the pitcher, robbing him of his voice and his strength so completely that Zephon was removed from the game. We knew in the dream the game had changed and this pitcher would never pitch again."

So get this: when the Red Sea parted, Israel passed through safely at the very place they were most exposed, most vulnerable, most weak. At Baal-Zephon, squeezed against a wall of water with no escape, God made them truly free. On the other side of the Zephon crisis, they gained a new and deeper understanding of God's ways and power, such that Pharaoh – the king who had enslaved them for centuries – forever lost his strength, power and voice over their fate. Never again would Pharaoh control them. Though he had thought to strike down Israel once and for all, he instead was removed from the game. The just reward of his rebellion against Yahweh was a sea full of the chariots, horses and corpses of his once mighty army. No wonder the Israelites boasted so greatly in their God when they realized His fierce and brilliant salvation. Listen to the hymn they sang:

> *"The LORD is a man of war;*
> **the LORD is his name…**
> **Your right hand, O LORD, glorious in power,**
> **your right hand, O LORD, shatters the enemy…**
> *Who is like you, O LORD, among the gods?*
> **Who is like you, majestic in holiness, awesome in glorious deeds, doing wonders?"** (Exo. 15:3, 6, 11)

We need to be done with pacifist notions of serving a lesser god who just wants peace at any cost. Yahweh is committed to total victory, enforcing peace over every enemy on behalf of His people. His methodology does not involve *any* negotiation, appeasement, concessions or toleration of the enemy. Zero. Thus, if you read the Exodus rightly, you will see that, in one sense, the

Red Sea is the necessary, logical conclusion to the Passover. One could almost say that where Passover broke the gods of Egypt, the Red Sea broke Pharaoh. For our purpose, Pharaoh represents the alignment of oppressive human power structures with corrupt principalities. God similarly intends to bring total deliverance in heaven and on earth. That's why we read in Jeremiah 50:25,

> **"The LORD has *opened his armory***
> ***and brought out the weapons* of his wrath,**
> **for the Lord GOD of hosts has a work to do"**

How advanced is the weaponry stored in the arsenal of heaven? Do you think part of God's navigation of history might include an unfolding, progressive revelation (and restoration) of tools He's already put in our hands? In chapter nine, we'll see the great battle at the end of the age framed by the heavenly contest to bring down the accuser of the brethren. There, the saints overcome by **"the blood of the lamb and the word of their testimony."** So while our voice – our testimony – is guaranteed to grow stronger, by contrast the enemy's accusations, intimidations and lies will one day be silenced forever. The waters of the Red Sea will once again cover the armies of hell. Since the Garden, Satan's power has always been in his voice, but one day soon he will lose all the power his lies have maintained over our thoughts, over history itself.

I believe every time we take Communion, we have the potential to further reduce his voice, both in our lives and in the world around us.

That's why, to fully glean from this dream, we must see the convergence of the biblical narrative embedded in the symbols. Dutch pulled the bat *"from a large wooden Communion box* where it had been locked inside." Furthermore, the bat was inscribed with Ephesians 1:17, the verse where Paul prayed for believers to continually receive **"the Spirit of wisdom and of revelation in the knowledge of Him."**

There is power in Communion to strike the throat – that vile breath-and-voice-box – of Baal, god of Baal-zephon. Furthermore, if we rightly discern our times, I believe we are meant to see the Passover decade of the 2020s as God structuring multiple confrontations with Pharaoh – the Egypt system, Harlot Babylon, occultic powers, antichrist governments and wicked world systems – with strike after strike after strike. He wants to put a weapon in our hands, drawn from His armory for the great work of cleansing the earth of evil. The rabbis see Passover as the time Pharaoh gets punched in the mouth so that his tooth is knocked out. In the dream, Zephon was struck in the throat so that his voice was removed. These are the same pictures.

Also, we must not miss that the weapon employed, the baseball bat, was pulled from a Communion box with a spirit of wisdom and revelation carved into it. In baseball terms, you use a bat to strike the ball. In other words, the only way to win is to take a swing! Begin experimenting with Communion with an extra measure of creativity and faith. Add aggressive, overcoming prayers, resistance prayers, triumphant prayers to your meal of bread and wine.

Lastly, the fact that Dutch (a man known for depths of understanding in intercession) received this weapon, and for

Ephesians 1:17 to be the verse, means we are meant to grow both in the way we handle this tool, and in the intercessory act that Communion represents.

Communion *is* prophetic activism. It is literally reenacting the triumph of the blood. It does more than demonstrate gratitude, it invokes the very presence of Christ among us. It does more than connect us to an emotion of penitence, reverence or hope, it wildly boasts, **"The LORD is a man of war; the LORD is his name! Your right hand shatters the enemy! Who is like you, O LORD, among the gods?"**

communion reconfirms the castrated, impotent state of our enemy. he may roar, but his tooth has been knocked out

Communion reconfirms the castrated, impotent state of our enemy. He may roar, but his tooth has been knocked out. When you participate in the mysterious, sacramental grace of Communion, the damnable lies and accusations of Satan fall silent. You are hidden in Christ, covered by the power of His blood.

NOTES & REFLECTIONS

chapter 6

THE SHIELD WALL OF HISTORY

"Do not limit the power of the blood of Christ to what you understand."

W.B. Young, *Honor the Blood*[19]

The Great Communion Revival

Many years ago, I had a dream in which I vividly saw the great harvest at the end of the age. Over a series of events that occurred earlier in the dream, I had been used to set off a nuclear bomb which, rather than producing destruction on earth, instead sent shockwaves of cleansing power into the upper atmosphere, clearing the skies of contamination and darkness. After the atomic plume faded, the sky became a giant movie screen, permitting the gospel to be declared around the world with undeniable power. As the most dramatic movie of redemption played out across the entire sky, end to end in every city and nation, I knew this global witness was a sign and a wonder that would sweep a billion souls into the kingdom.

Notice that *after* the skies had been cleared, people could see and think clearly. They simply knew they needed Jesus. The systematic web of lies and false ideologies that had held them captive for so long was finally broken. In the dream, I wept.

It was so powerful, so moving. Miracles and salvation began happening everywhere. It was a breakthrough moment in human history. Still weeping, I woke at precisely 3:16 am. **"For God so loved the world"** (John 3:16).

I tell the story of this dream in detail in *The Jesus Fast*, but in the years since writing that book with Lou, I have begun to wonder whether Communion is also part of the story. In other words, how do we clear the skies? Part of the answer is fasting. I believe both Scripture and history point to fasting as a great, untapped resource, like an undetonated bomb. We need to drop more nuclear fasting bombs – extended seasons of fasting and prayer for personal and corporate breakthrough. The Lord has been stirring more and more across the world to enter into the labor and grace of fasting with prayer, and I believe we will see more and more breakthrough in hard, dark places as a result.

But one thing has always troubled me. In my dream, as a bomb engineer, I actually had *two bombs* to detonate. In my own small way, publishing *The Jesus Fast* was an attempt to detonate one of them. But having come to understand more of the cosmic dimensions of the Lord's Table, I see now how taking the elements with faith can turn a meal of bread and wine into a devastatingly effective intercessory act capable of equal or greater disruptive, dislodging power in the second heavens.

If fasting taps into nuclear spiritual power, the Cross is thermonuclear. There is simply nothing in our arsenal to compare.

If true, the problem is not whether we are adequately resourced for victory, but whether we have the revelation and resolve to actively deploy what God has literally put into our hands. Satan has been defeated, but still retains "squatter's rights" over the earth. The ongoing problem of evil in the world is proof that while God has **"put everything in subjection to him (and) left nothing outside his control…at present,** *we do not yet see everything in subjection* **to him"** (Hebrews 2:8). Though squatter's rights are not actually a legitimate land claim, they do represent a recognized form of occupation and control that results from the abdication or absence of the legal enforcement and residency of the *true* owner.

As the Body of Christ and the ekklesia of Jesus, we need to begin delivering eviction notices in the second heavens. I am not content to let the pharaohs of earth and sky hold people in bondage. We need massive, global breakthrough.

We need Passover again.

A couple of years ago, Lou's son, Josiah, had an interesting dream that coincides with my dream. Josiah saw that Lou was going to address the nation somehow, either over a news broadcast or in the form of a *movie*. As Lou discussed his message with another person in the dream, he asked them, 'What should I tell the nation?' The other person replied, "Show them the broken bread. *That's the buster."*

In the dream, Josiah knew that the broken bread was Communion, and the 'buster' was a blockbuster. What is a blockbuster movie? *It's a movie that everybody sees.* Josiah knew that the blockbuster of Communion would break through to reach the most people. While not exactly the same as mine, I found Josiah's dream remarkably similar in spirit to what I saw. In my dream, after the nuclear bomb had cleared the skies, the skies themselves became a movie screen where *everyone saw,* both believer and unbeliever alike.

You Are the Movie Screen

Follow this. It's incredible. The Apostle Paul's great manifesto on the ekklesia (the church) is found in Ephesians. Brimming with profound, almost exhausting language that develops our corporate mission, calling and purpose, Ephesians is considered the high water mark of ecclesiology. In the first chapter, Paul prays both for the believers in Ephesus and for every generation of the ekklesia that, **"Having** *the eyes of your hearts enlightened…***that you may know what is the hope to which he has called you, what are** *the riches of his glorious inheritance in the saints"* (Ephesians 1:18)

The key word to this transformative process, the means by which the Holy Spirit helps us understand the hope of our calling and the riches of His glorious inheritance *in* us – US! – is for our hearts to be *enlightened*. The Greek word Paul uses is *'photizos'*, which is based on the root 'phos.' It means light or illumination. You can probably see that it is the word from which we derive our English word, *photo*graph.

Harkening back to the days before Photoshop when light-sensitive physical film was developed in a darkroom, our inner darkroom must be illumined with the light of Christ until our whole being is filled with light. By definition, this means old, false Polaroids based on lies, bad theology, stale tradition and experience that have a form of godliness but deny its power must be replaced with true knowledge of the Logos, apprehended by faith. You can be saved and still view the purpose of God with darkened or diminished understanding. Paraphrased, Paul's prayer is for "the eyes of our heart to be brought out of darkness into light!"

There is a glorious calling on your life. Christ has an impossibly rich inheritance in His ekklesia. His purpose for us and through us is huge. Can you believe that? If you tend to shrink the scale of it down to polite, manageable proportions, you probably need more light.

So when two chapters later Paul says it is through you and me – **"through the ekklesia"** – that the **"manifold wisdom of God"** is made known **"to the rulers and authorities in the heavenly place"** we must see that He is now pointing that light toward us for us to reflect back as a witness into heavenly places.

Picture it with Christ as the lens of the Father. As God the Son, Jesus focuses and reveals all that God is. Jesus said,

"Whoever has seen me has *seen* the Father" (John 14:9). Christ is **"the image of the invisible God"** and **"the fullness of God"** (Colossians 1:15, 19). Thus, like a movie projector positioned in the darkened theater of our depraved, warring planet, the source of light – **"the Father of light"** (James 1:17) – passes through the powerful, perfectly accurate lens of His Son to reveal God to earth.

Using this analogy, both the light and the lens are the divine source, but the lens focuses and refracts the Father's massive, brilliant, but hidden light into the darkness (**"to bring to light"** Ephesians 3:9). John explains it this way, **"In him was life, and the life was the light of men,"** then added that **"the light shines in the darkness"** (John 1:4-5).

Yet something is still missing. The light and the lens need a fixed object upon which, and through which, to reveal itself. In a movie theater, if the lens reveals the light, it is the screen that reveals the lens. Paul told the Corinthians that he and the other apostles, as humans, had been made **"a spectacle"** not only to men, but angels (1 Corinthians 4:9). That word, spectacle, is the Greek word, *'theatron'*, from which we get our word, theater.

And so it is! Thru the ekklesia, God not only reveals Christ to the world, but also proclaims the manifold wisdom of God to rulership structures in heavenly dimensions in the outer darkness. When the ekklesia assembles, the light of Christ concentrates on the movie screen of our lives, piercing the darkness. We would be wise to carefully curate the kind of movie we show. For my part, I want to display the riches of His glory in every way possible.

Beloved, there is no greater story than the Cross.

Paul's ecclesiology radically affirms man's governmental purpose (remember, he places the ekklesia in juxtaposition *against* **"rulers and authorities"**). Therefore, part of our high calling and great privilege is to be the movie screen of God. We would do well to make this part of the litmus test by which we judge whether we are on task or not. Is church attendance up or down? Was the offering good? These are secondary, possibly meaningless measures, yet have represented the sort of criteria by which "church" has judged its effectiveness for centuries.

No, no, no!

Are nations being discipled into the Kingdom? Are testimonies of righteousness, justice and mercy being illumined, flung into the darkness of this world? Are rebel principalities and powers being forced to behold the triumph of Christ and the power of His blood on the movie screen of our lives?

God considers you and me to be His *inheritance*. Can you imagine? But if we are His, He is certainly ours. Communion is part of how we practice that inheritance. Most Protestants have been blind and dull for too long to Communion's theatrical, experiential, transforming, demon-tormenting celebration of the atoning, delivering goodness of God. The elements tell a wild story in which God has made us active participants. We are causal agents of history, not bystanders, and certainly not victims.

Oh, we need the passion, ethos and triumph of this blockbuster to thunder in our souls once more. Beloved, get this! Get this light in you. If you lack, ask. The Body of Christ needs an infusion of *aha!* moments regarding the precious blood, the powerful blood, the Passover blood, the penetrating blood.

New Revelation Coming

To combine Josiah's dream with mine, I believe there is new light, new revelation, coming to the church. We're going to *see* the power of the gospel and the transmissive power of Communion. This will dramatically illuminate and expand our understanding of what Jesus literally put in our hands in the simple form of bread and wine, for this is not any bread and wine, but Christ! There is no bigger blockbuster than the radical, inexorable power of the gospel, and the eucharist gives us all a ticket to experience it over and over again.

> **there is no bigger blockbuster than the radical, inexorable power of the gospel, and the eucharist gives us all a ticket to experience it over and over again**

When Christians of every denomination enter into Communion with fresh and ever-expanding understanding, we'll see Christ crucified in a new light, bright as a projector in a darkened theater. The story will unfold anew in our hearts. But by participating in that process with a meal that celebrates the Man, I believe we will also begin to bear witness into invisible realms of darkness, focusing that same gospel brilliance like a billion candle-watt flashlight into every roach-infested corner of the planet.

Wherever demons love to hide, we are meant to draw bloodlines in the spirit (I'll discuss this more in chapters seven and eight). Communion not only turns the radical gospel into a meal of unfiltered, primal grace, it is meant to humble, beautify and deliver us from our pettiness, unforgiveness, bitterness and scorn, until "Father, forgive them!" becomes a united war cry for the salvation of the world.

Since that fateful night in 33 AD, Jesus has infused the elements with perpetual prophetic potential – stored energy – as if the elements have become magnetized to the Cross with such constant residual force that the power of the Cross can be released over and over again at any time when we decide to remember, proclaim, celebrate and reenact. Could it be?

If so, it is a buster indeed! Such a breakthrough power, regularly employed, might be like a smart missile continually bombarding demonic territories with the sure and certain pronouncement of their total defeat and future annihilation.

Prophetic activism is spiritually kinetic. Gestures, movements and commanded actions are neither empty, nor inert. In a sense, much as the Word of God, they live, imbued with something from another dimension. When we faithfully engage with the ritual, the symbol, the presence and the power – when we literally feed on the victory of the Cross – we are becoming conduits, millions of times over, for that decisive victory to be replayed, power to be released, and a message be proclaimed. Demons cannot help but shudder, falter and fail; and the world cannot help but notice.

Clearing the Skies

In another dream, Josiah saw President Eisenhower in a time of war marshaling a massive assault force – multiple brigades and divisions, including infantry, intelligence, airborne, engineering, medical and more – for an epic invasion. In the dream,

Eisenhower was reviewing the battle plan and rallying his men when he boldly declared, "You are about to hear the clashing of swords on the shield wall of history!"

This is precise dream language, and should not be overlooked. A shield wall is a classic defensive formation from antiquity. Whether the opposing army was advancing by force on the ground, or by a volley of arrows from the air, a shield wall interlocked the shield of the soldiers to form a monolithic wall of resistance.

As you will remember, Eisenhower was the Supreme Commander of the Allied Forces during World War 2, responsible for leading the the largest amphibious invasion in military history. The assault on Normandy by water, land and air, codenamed Operation Overlord – what we now call D-Day – was the critical, costly turning point of WWII. One year later, May 7, 1945, Germany surrendered. What a fitting picture of the Lord of Hosts commanding the armies of heaven and earth for the recapture of the planet! But it will not come without resistance. As previously discussed in chapter two, the Psalm 2 and Psalm 82 conspiracy of kings and false gods against the rightful claim of Christ upon His own planet is increasingly forming a shield wall of resistance to the advance of the kingdom. This is an act of desperation because they know their time is short.

At a certain level, this is proof of the times in which we live and the terror the enemy feels. Satan seeks to resist our advance, but the Lord has weapons in His armory too powerful for him to resist. On the other hand, it also means we must get comfortable with conflict, spiritual warfare, and therefore better versed in the authority we possess. The King of Heaven is raising His government (the ekklesia) to dislodge every interloper, every guerilla force, every fortified bunker or Banana Republic of hell on earth. The Healer is removing every toxin. The Deliverer is coming to deliver and the Christ is coming to rule and reign.

But this is not a unilateral process.

The Spirit of God has determined to raise up sons and daughters of stature and strength, of overcoming, persevering obedience, and of sacrificial intervention. He is not only coming back, He is bringing us *with* Him by transforming us *to* Him. Heaven is actively ripening the sons of the Kingdom by accelerating the grace available for us to come to a place of maturity where we are well-trained, highly effective intercessory instruments in His hands. We are learning to rule from places above, not below.

> **"He made my feet like the feet of a deer**
> **and set me secure on the heights.**
> ***He trains my hands for war,* so that**
> **my arms can bend a bow of bronze"** (Psalm 18:33-34)

Do you know your place? You are either part of that advance force landing on the beaches of Normandy, charging the enemy's ranks to establish beachheads for further advancement, or you are part of the next wave of occupiers that proceed to relentlessly displace and resettle the ravaged territories where the hunkered forces of the enemy still seek to govern and control. Left unchallenged, the squatter troops of the enemy will not relent. But we have a weapon! It's the weapon by which they have already been judged: the blood of Christ.

This brings me back to the idea of Communion essentially raising the blood as a witness to the powers of lawlessness in the second heaven. Paul said that it was through the ekklesia that **"the manifold wisdom of God might** *now be made known to the rulers and authorities in the heavenly places"* (Ephesians 3:10). Paul then goes on to say that in Christ we have **"boldness and** *access with confidence* **through our faith in Him"** (vs. 12).

In the context of the preceding verses, Paul has prophetically defined a mandate which the ekklesia of Christ is meant to accomplish. It involves, unity together, love, and confident access to His presence. Note, every one of these are an intended biblical result of taking Communion. While certainly not exclusive to Communion, the result of anything that transforms the ekklesia into this exalted status achieves a certain result: the witness of the wisdom of God being made known to wicked powers in heavenly dimensions.

Paul told the believers in Corinth that **"the saints will judge the world"** and, one day, **"judge angels"** (2 Corinthians 6:2-3). You get to practice that now. D-Day was followed by V-Day. The invasion led to victory. Imagine if a time traveler could have begun broadcasting V-Day during the final year of the war. Imagine the certainty of the outcome being broadcast to not only humiliate and demoralize the enemy, but in a sense to weaken their capacity for the fight. Communion is the blockbuster we display behind enemy lines, containing both the certitude of the victory of Christ in His first coming and the devastating certainty of His return.

I half imagine that when we take Communion in the way the Lord desires, angels are released to corral unruly spirits into a darkened place and make them watch the movie over and over, the one where we become the participant re-enactors of Calvary's conquest.

A little known prophecy from the prophet, Micah, promises that the days of the Exodus are coming again.

> **"Shepherd your people…as in the days of old.**
> *As in the days when you came out of the land of Egypt,*
> *I will show them marvelous things"* (Micah 7:14-15)

Since the days of the original Exodus, history has never again witnessed such a staggering sequence of supernatural events, nor such a visible clash of spiritual powers, as when Israel was brought out of Egypt. Micah is unequivocal: it's coming again. But whereas the Exodus with Israel was limited to one tiny region of the earth, the clash of kingdoms in the last days will be global in scale. Zephaniah similarly prophesies God's intention. He's in it to win.

> **"The LORD will be awesome against them;** *for he*
> *will famish all the gods* **of the earth"** (Zephaniah 2:11).

If you don't understand what's happening, it's easy to lose heart. Why is the earth groaning so deeply under the surging (resurgence?) of dark powers?

In his remarkable book, *The Return of the Gods,* author Jonathan Cahn warns that the gods of Mesopotamia never died, they were simply exorcised from the culture of Israel by the power of Christ over the period of 30-33 AD. From there, slowly but inexorably over the ensuing centuries, Christianity expanded across Palestine, then Europe, then into the New World. History records the expanding triumph of the gospel as the displacement of the old gods and old worship systems across all those territories. This was not only a result of personal salvation, but the transformation of culture. The power of God's love and redemption by the atoning work of Christ caused the polytheism and pantheism of the Greco-Roman world to surrender to the superior message of gospel. Over many decades and centuries, nation after nation became unshackled from the dark spell of the gods they had once served. Over time, however, if those nations turn from the God that delivered them, their civilization stands at great risk of an even worse process of re-demonization.

Cahn makes the point that this is precisely what Jesus indicated in Matthew 12:

> **"When an unclean spirit goes out of a man, he goes through dry places, seeking rest, and finds none. Then he says, 'I will return to my house from which I came.' And when he comes, he finds it empty, swept, and put in order. Then he goes and takes with him seven other spirits more wicked than himself, and they enter and dwell there; and the last state of that man is worse than the first.** *So shall it also be with this wicked generation*" (Matthew 12:43–45, NKJV).

That is to say, the exorcism of demonic powers is not only a personal event, it is a cultural imperative. The downside is that this raises the same risk for civilization as for the individual: *re*possession of a worse kind than the original state. When those nations that were once delivered, cleaned and put in order are found empty by turning from the God who first put their house in order, the door opens for the gods to return with vengeance.

Prior to Christ, Israel repeatedly typified this dangerous cycle of apostasy and renewal, therefore we can learn a great lesson from its most vigilant reformer.

Josiah the Reformer

Like a codebook interpreting clues, a dreamer and their dream can sometimes offer interlocking insights, especially when a relevant biblical story can be connected to a name in the dream, or in this case, of the dreamer. In that sense, I believe the name of Lou's son, Josiah, should harken our imagination back to King Josiah, the most radical reformer and faithful king in the checkered history of Judah. Prior to Josiah, under his wicked father, King Amon, and even more under his grandfather, Manasseh (perhaps the second most wicked king of Judah, of whom it was said he did **"things more evil than all that the Amorites,"** 2 Kings 21:11), the land had fallen into gross darkness, occultism, depravity and the shedding of innocent blood.

After Josiah assumed the crown at the tender age of eight years old, somewhere around 621 BC, he launched a program of national renewal across the Souther Kingdom. The Temple was refurbished, purged of foreign priests and false idols, then rededicated wholly to the worship of Yahweh. Pagan shrines were desecrated and destroyed, cultic sacrifices to other gods were stopped, including Baal, Asherah, Chemosh, Milcom and "all the host of heaven", while the lost scrolls of the Law of Moses were recovered and read again in the hearing of the people.

Interestingly, it was during this time of deep spiritual renewal, under the leadership of a king who bravely challenged the squatter gods, that we also see the dramatic reinstatement of Passover at a level previously unseen for centuries.

> "**And** *the king commanded all the people, 'Keep the Passover to the LORD your God,* **as it is written in this Book of the Covenant.'** *For no such Passover had been kept since* **the days of the judges who judged Israel, or during all the days of the kings of Israel or of the kings of Judah…**
>
> *Before him there was no king like him, who turned to the LORD with all his heart and with all his soul and with all his might,* **according to all the Law of Moses, nor did any like him arise after him."** (1 Kings 23:21-22, 25)

More than any other king in ancient Israel, Josiah was like a young Eisenhower, storming the beachhead of darkness in Israel.

Walking the Road with the Lamb of God

Beloved, are you beginning to see? That is the question: Do. You. See? As never before, we must see Christ; Communion is critical to washing and opening our eyes, strengthening our vision, lifting our gaze. In fact, for two disciples who were dull and blind, the act of Communion did precisely that. On a road called Emmaus, their eyes were opened.

> **"While they were talking and discussing together, Jesus himself drew near and went with them.** *But their eyes were kept from recognizing him."*

This is fascinating, but loaded with insight. Though its truly Jesus, even disciples who once knew Him *couldn't see Him in His resurrection power*. Once upon a time, they had known Him one way, but for whatever reason, they lacked the ability to recognize Him in His victorious new body. Thinking He was someone else, He was still so wise and compelling in his understanding of Scripture that when they finally arrived at Emmaus, they pressed Him to stay so they could keep asking questions. There was much to learn and (hidden) Jesus was teaching them all about Himself from Scripture. Can you imagine such a thing? Later,

> **"When he was at table with them, he took the bread and blessed and broke it and gave it to them.** *And their eyes were opened, and they recognized him…* **They said to each other, 'Did not our hearts burn within us while he talked to us on the road, while he opened to us the Scriptures?'"** (Luke 24:15-16, 30-32)

After this, Jesus simply disappeared from their sight. Shocked, the two immediately made the seven mile trek back to Jerusalem where they bore witness to the other troubled disciples that Christ was, indeed, resurrected. **They told what had happened on the road, and** *how he was known to them in the breaking of the bread* (v. 33).

Somehow, I believe this is where we are right now. There are dimensions of Christ in His resurrected power and glory that we have failed to fully comprehend. I don't know if we've lost it over the generations, or if He is adding new understanding that the Body of Christ has never attained, but for which, in the fullness of time, we are now appointed to receive. This, too, is part of the Great Communion Revival. What have we not recognized in Christ that Communion is meant to disclose to us? These promises and prophecies, these whispers and dreams, are stirring our proverbial blood in more ways than one.

Worldwide, I believe God desires to put His people back on the road to Emmaus. He wants our eyes to open, our hearts to burn. There are ways we have seen Him that are too limited to who He was before the Cross, instead of *after* the Cross.

Altars and Wells

As I close this chapter, I'll share one more dream from Chris Berglund. Chris saw the same altar that Elijah had built in 1 Kings 18, but this time it was covered with a high priestly robe. The robe was laid on top of it like a tablecloth. He saw the 12 stones of the High Priestly robe, representing the 12 tribes, and also knew the altar itself was made of the same 12 stones. On top of this were laid the Communion elements. The altar of Elijah was literally the Table of the Lord.

He saw the elements of bread and wine, but the bread kept switching between being a loaf and a lamb. From that scene, Chris looked out and saw restored altars of God all across the land, covered in white tablecloths with Communion elements on top.

He heard a phrase: "Building altars, opening wells."

Then the dream ended.

This precisely pictures what I believe God is doing in this hour. In the Great Communion Revival, the Holy Spirit is restoring our awe, while also expanding the purpose and utility of Communion in our hearts. As in the dream with Dutch, we are learning to strike with it. As in the dream above, we are learning to make it an altar of His presence. As in the two dreams of Josiah, we are learning supernatural dimensions of the power of the blood of the Lamb to terrorize and demoralize the enemy, and restore our land. We are spreading altars across our nations, building altars in our homes. As prophetic activism, Communion imposes deep, fearful realities upon the resistant forces of heavenly realms.

Perhaps our blood has been weak, and perhaps we have lived anemically, yet in the grace of God, we're on the road to Emmaus again. Our gaze is once more upon the Lamb on the throne, He who sits in triumph at the center of the universe. We follow the one found worthy to open the scroll and to break the seven seals of history. He alone will receive the full inheritance He deserves among the peoples of the earth.

This harkens back to the rally cry of one of the greatest prayer movements in history. When the Moravians of Herrnhut, Germany, began to send missionaries to the furthest reaches of the earth in the early 1800s (even selling themselves into slavery to reach slaves who would otherwise never hear the gospel), the young men would push back from shore with all their earthly belongings packed in a coffin. Assuming they would not live to see their families again, they would raise their voices as they departed, crying out, "That the Lamb may receive the reward of his suffering!"

The Moravian battle cry must be raised once more:

"All glory to the Lamb!"

SECTION TAKEAWAYS

1. Leviticus offers powerful insights into the doctrine of blood. By gravely defining the need for a priesthood and sacrificial system as requirements of a holy God, we are left with no doubt about the consequences of sin under the Law.

2. The futility of achieving righteousness under the Law is meant to convince us of the superior life we are offered in Christ. We are not to mix the two, but to fully embrace the Holy Spirit's transforming work under the terms of the new covenant, which is a product of faith, not works.

3. The template for lasting revival is to be found only in a radical embrace of the new covenant. As such, the 2020s are a decade for the Body of Christ to receive fresh revelation not only of the Passover story, but of Passover history being relieved in our day, and how Communion becomes a means for us to embrace and prophetically demonstrate the power of Jesus' blood to speak a better word.

4. God is raising up spiritual reformers like Josiah, the young king of Israel, to bring transformation to societies that are becoming re-demonized through the neglect of God's word and ways. The "shield wall of history" will be breached by the saints for the glory of the Lamb.

BETTER BLOOD

chapter 7

INHERITANCE, MARKERS & SIGNS

"In a symbol THERE IS CONCEALMENT AND YET REVELATION…the Infinite is made to blend itself with the Finite and stand visible."[20]

Thomas Carlyle

As we meditate on the purpose and function of blood for its theological implications, its diverse metaphorical potential, its mystical power, or merely as a needful component of biology and medicine, we discover that blood never loses its sense of vitality or meaning.

This chapter will examine two of those metaphorical and theological categories:

1. How bloodlines denote spiritual lineage, therefore offer keys to inheritance
2. How literal lines of blood in Scripture uniquely mark a story or point to other divine activity

There is no way around the simple fact that *His story* is marked with blood. For this reason, I too want to stamp us with this thought: *blood lines matter*. My goal is that by exploring these two blood lines we can all meditate more deeply upon the power of the blood to point to Christ. Then, perhaps we can be poised to experience Communion as an eschatological mark upon our lives and homes, by which the entire Body of Christ can be equipped and anointed for the challenging, glorious days ahead.

1. Keys to Inheritance (Spiritual Lineage)

History, as the record of nations and kings, has constantly focused on the respective attempts of various noblemen to establish their own dynastic bloodlines. Wars have been fought over which heir to which throne had the most legitimate claim.

As a source of evil, racism succeeds only by falsely distorting the inherent value of one ethnic bloodline above another. Because bloodlines are intuitively important, the claims of racism rise to dark levels of spiritual authority.

On a more personal level, families are built on bloodlines established by the covenant of marriage and the transference of DNA, wealth and various privileges built by one generation and passed to another. Blood establishes family lines in the Spirit, too. The blood of Jesus defines your relationship to Him.

Public fascination with genealogies has been given renewed attention by various online ancestry research services. Personally, I've given weeks to researching my own family history. I found myself fascinated by how that journey opened up a world of previously untapped personal identity. For example, though I am anything but natural royalty in the modern sense, I discovered that I have direct connections to the first Norman kings of England and also Scotland's Robert the Bruce. It struck me with a sort of profundity to discover that these men were in *my* bloodline!

Though centuries have passed, in some sense, they live on in me. The very thought inspires a measure of desire to continue their legacy of courage and valor, or at least to make a similarly notable imprint on history. Some may dismiss that as vainglorious, but I see it as the inheritance of a bloodline. And that's the point! Knowing that my roots sink centuries deep into the soil of history, into real men and women who truly shaped history, somehow gives me a better sense of my own place in the world and the level of aspiration with which I choose to live.

The Bible gives great attention to genealogy, as well. We know because most of us skip over it. But it was quite important in establishing the Messiah's bloodline. If Jesus were to inherit

David's throne, He had to be provably descended from David's lineage. If the Bible pays attention, so should we.

Does Communion reshape itself in your soul to realize the ritual is, in one sense, ancestral at the highest spiritual level? In sharing His blood, you prove yourself part of a bloodline.

One of the most famous and influential rabbis of all time was Moses ben Maimon, commonly called Maimonides (the acronym of his full name spells 'Rambam'). In expounding upon one of Maimonides insights, Tanakh lecturer, Rabbi Alex Israel, wrote,

> "For the Rambam, the blood on the doorposts is a test of faith for the Jews in Egypt. By giving Yisrael the ritual of the Passover (Pesach) lamb. God has entered the picture and has presented them with an ultimatum. This is how it works. The Egyptians claim that if the Israelites slaughter the sheep, they will bring ruin upon themselves. The gods will be angered…Hashem is telling Yisrael that the only way they will survive (is) if they do slaughter the lamb, barbecuing it and daubing its blood on their doorways.
>
> What does an assimilated Egyptian Jew do in such a situation? This must have been quite a dilemma. According to the Rambam that was the precise objective of the exercise! The night of Passover was the night of choice: Do you want to be a Jew or an Egyptian? Do you follow the God of the Israelites or the gods of Egypt? Tonight is the showdown. If you do not take the lamb, you will be an Egyptian. Whoever does take the lamb will be a Jew.
>
> Now, let us not imagine that the choice was easy. They had to paint the blood on their doorposts. They had to

mark themselves!...*So the act of taking the lamb and daubing its blood on ones front door, is in fact an act of identification... The Pesach lamb proclaims a message; 'I will not be an Egyptian. My destiny lies with the God of Israel'.*"[21]

Consider that if marking homes with blood was a necessary distinction, what might it mean for the people themselves to be marked with blood? As we have seen, blood contained the essence of life in Jewish thought. It was commanded not to be eaten, but was instead reserved for the priests, who returned it to God by pouring it on the altar (Leviticus 17).

With this in mind, a passage from Exodus 24 presents itself with a certain degree of strangeness. Firstly, Moses, not Aaron, is seen presiding over a particular sacrifice of bulls. Secondly, while Moses throws half the blood onto the altar, as expected, he throws the other half onto the people. At least according to Leviticus 17, that action is *not* to be expected.

This ritual was a marking ritual. As Moses proclaimed "Behold the blood of the covenant that the Lord has made with you concerning all these words" he sprinkled or flung droplets of blood into the crowd, rather than properly presenting them on the altar.

Imagine this strange, grim scene, and you might recoil unless you put symbol with symbol in the whole counsel of God to see instead how Yahweh brilliantly employed a highly visual ritual to make sure Israel connected *themselves* to God's redemptive story.

Here's what I mean. If the altar is where the blood belongs, and if blood is meant to effect an initiation, then *putting the blood on the people turned them into an altar.*

This ritual created a blood community not by virtue of their shared descent from Abraham's bloodline, but because of the covenantal, sacrificial blood sprinkled upon them, primitively marking each individual as a prototype of the living sacrifice we are meant to be. The collective became the very altar of God.

Under the terms of our new and better covenant, the blood of Christ touches us directly, not by proxy. It works internally and invisibly to regenerate and reconnect our spirit to God. His blood redefines our identity as we become the very bloodline of Christ, sons and coheirs with Him to the Father of all.

> **For this reason I bow my knees before the Father,** *from whom every family in heaven and on earth is named,* **that according to the riches of His glory He may grant you to be strengthened with power through His Spirit in your inner being, so that Christ may dwell in your hearts through faith – that you,** *being rooted and grounded in love,* **may have strength to comprehend with all the saints what is the breadth and length and height and depth, and to know the love of Christ that surpasses knowledge, that you may be filled with all the fullness of God.** (Ephesians 3:14-19)

2. Narrative markers

Having looked at several blood narratives already – Passover being the most predominant – two additional stories will briefly serve to make the point of how blood has been used in Scripture to metaphorically point our attention in certain directions, either to help us gain a deeper insight or at minimum, to not overlook the main point. Narratively speaking, blood of this sort becomes a kind of code. It achieves the same thing a street sign, a highway billboard, or a blinking neon indicator might: Look here, it says, there's a message inside. Look closer, don't miss it!

The famous battle between David and Goliath is one such example. During a trip to Israel a few years back I had the good fortune to visit the very location described in Scripture, and to this day it remains identifiable exactly as the Bible describes it. The area is distinguished by two long ridges that face one another with a broad plain in between. It is a perfect battlefield. The ridges are steep and the field is flat, but a wet weather stream flows through it that is frequently dry enough to easily cross, from which David could quickly grab five smooth stones.

At first, the place names given for the area seem like unnecessary details or cartographical filler until we realize they actually form bullet points for a simple, profound takeaway. We are told that Israel was:

> **"...encamped between Socoh and Azekah, in Ephes-dammim. And Saul and the men of Israel were gathered, and encamped in the Valley of Elah, and drew up in line of battle against the Philistines. And the Philistines stood on the mountain on the one side, and Israel stood on the mountain on the other side, with a valley between them."** (1 Samuel 17:1-3)

You know the rest.

Every day for forty days, Goliath would come down from the ridge, down into the field, raise his booming voice and challenge any man of Israel to similarly come down and fight him. He would taunt, boast and curse. He would insult God. In so doing, he terrorized the puny Israelites, who cowered in fear on the ridge, afraid for their lives. Goliath eventually offered total victory, meaning the enslavement of the entire Philistine army, should any Israelite champion be able to best him. Nobody dared. Every man in Israel was too busy shaking in their boots. Why?

Because they judged Goliath according to the flesh. Viewed in his natural might, given the limitations of their own natural strength, none of the 5'5" inch Israelites wanted to face a warrior who stood 9-12 feet tall, fully armored in bronze and wielding a giant spear. King Saul, who was noted as being the tallest man among all the armies of Israel (therefore the most natural opponent) had no interest in the fight.

So let's look at this. For two opposing armies to face each other from two opposing mountains speaks of two kingdoms in conflict. The natural therefore speaks to the spiritual. Goliath is a type of the accuser of the brethren because he wears them down over forty days of testing, not only with his imposing stature but more specifically with threats, intimidations and curses. He accused them!

Furthermore, technically, since this land belonged to Judah, we are meant to understand that the enemy had clearly made inroads into the Promised Land. Lastly, the story subtly suggests the reason for these encroachments: Saul's cowardly leadership. (I want to encourage you to practice reading Scripture in this way, not just at a surface level, but reading between the lines. Engage the text emotionally and creatively. Turn it into a conversation with God. There is always *always* more than meets the eye.)

David, the hero, had no physical stature to speak of. Though Scripture described him as handsome, this was no beauty contest. David was totally unimpressive and unintimidating to Goliath. He had nothing going for him in the natural. But!

David *did* operate under an anointing put upon him by the prophet Samuel in a previous chapter. He trusted in the power of God, not the flesh, professing the name of God as more potent than the taunts of Goliath. He told Goliath **"the battle (belongs) to the Lord"** (v. 47).

Finally, David lived in full confidence of Israel's covenant with Yahweh. He calls Goliath an "uncircumcised Philistine" which was David's way of saying, "I am a son of covenant, you are not. And *that* will be your undoing. My God will fight for me."

Like drawing water from a well, what nourishment and strength are we to draw from these insights? Firstly, the challenges of life will always force us to choose whether we will lean on our natural strength or walk in the ways of the Spirit. But this begs the question: what are those ways? Where does the young champion find his footing? If similar battle lines come to all of us, and we must pick a side, ask yourself: where will you draw your "line in the sand?"

Many additional instructions for life could be gleaned from this story, but I want to focus on that line. Where is the *line* that simultaneously brought David to the brink of destiny and Goliath to the place of defeat? Remember, nothing in Scripture is accidental. Every word is divinely inspired. So by pointing us to the anointed king, the one from whom Messiah will eventually come, is to point us to an early prototype of the Lion of the Tribe of Judah. David rushes to the field with a boast in the power of Yahweh's covenant, but he does so in a particular place.

It is the Valley of Elah, in the area of Ephes-*dammim*.

If you were paying attention in the last chapter, you probably already took note of that word. There it is again, the Hebrew root, '*dam*', the plural form of which is '*dammim*'.

Ephes-Dammin means "boundary of blood."

David positioned himself for victory at the boundary of blood. The son of covenant chose a boundary of blood to make his triumphant stand against his gigantic, satanic adversary.

> **the son of covenant chose a boundary of blood to make his triumphant stand against his satanic adversary**

If you are under the blood of Jesus, the boundary line appointed for victory is the boundary of His blood. There and there alone you must take your stand.

King of Glory

The most important blood lines are found in Scripture, but sometimes dreams draw blood lines, serving in the same fashion as pointers back to Scripture for further insight. As I said at the beginning, *this is a book of dreams*. Privately and publicly, Lou Engle fondly quotes Joel 2 and Acts to make a simple, often overlooked point, that dreams are the "last days language of heaven." What if we (and thousands more) are receiving dreams not merely as oracles or messages but as communicants of God's own longings? What if God is saying, "Here's what I dream about!" How would that change our perspective?

So in 2022, another Communion dream seemingly pointed once more to the urgency of that year (remember "It all adds up to 2022!"). A good friend and faithful intercessor dreamed he was sitting next to a man whose last name was Lyon. (We just saw a prototype of the Lion of Judah in action, right? In young David? Don't ignore word play and puns in your dreams. Pay attention to details like names, colors, locations, and signs, as they often add richness and depth to your dream or might even be key to the dream's central point.)

In the dream, my friend was getting ready to take Mr. Lyon out for breakfast, but he had a very concerned look on his face. In real life, Mr. Lyon had been profoundly influential as a discerning mentor and friend to the man having the dream, having taught him for years how to deeply meditate on the Lord and listen to His voice. So when Mr. Lyon spoke gravely, the dreamer knew this was symbolic of the Lord's own voice. He said, "You only have an hour to prepare for the Communion service."

He then added, "Remember, Christ the King of Glory inhabits a revelation of Himself."

In other words, this thing is about to quickly ramp up. Are you ready? (We weren't.) But just like children counting down for Hide and Seek, at some point the seeker cries out, "Ready or not, here I come!" So it is, these dreams were ways of getting the countdown in our soul. Ready or not, here He comes!

I want to say with boldness and humility, the days of Communion as empty ritual are coming to a close. Days of deep

Communion are more and more going to be the *life blood* (there it is!) of the *ekklesia* (the church). The dream assures us that while more revelation is coming, three things immediately stand out.

1. The true service and purpose of Communion is urgent on God's heart. We need to begin making adjustments.
2. Since the tribe of Judah was the tribe of royalty and worship in Israel, for a "lion" to give this warning may represent a divine summons for the Body of Christ to begin experiencing Communion as an act of worship beyond what most Protestants typically expect
3. Connected to this is the idea that ongoing "revelation" of "the King of Glory" is meant to be part of our experience of Communion Who is this King of Glory? Obviously, Psalm 24 holds the answer.

> **"Lift up your heads, O gates!**
> **And be lifted up, O ancient doors,**
> **that the King of glory may come in.**
> *Who is this King of glory?*
> *The LORD, strong and mighty,*
> *the LORD, mighty in battle!"* (Psalms 24:7-8)

Doors of history are not meant to hinder God, they are meant to swing wide. Doors of churches, locked in tradition, locked by governmental mandates, locked in small thinking – swing wide! Gates of Hades, be warned. You are meant to face the penetrating power of the gospel. Swing wide! Portals of heavenly power intended to release fresh anointing, new insights and divine power, swing wide! Locked up souls who are waiting to hear the message of Christ and receive salvation, swing wide!

The King of Glory has a revelation of Himself, and He inhabits (is present, ready, near) when we see Him as a strong warrior, mighty in battle, ready to vanquish and overcome everything that hinders love and raise up His people from despair and shame into their full destiny.

Red Stripe Road

During this ceremony transporting the Ark from Obed Edom's house to David's new Tabernacle, we are told that David sacrificed an ox and a fattened calf every six paces (2 Sam. 6:13). Though the precise location (and therefore distance) is not certain, the likely range is 1-6 miles. Such a trail of blood and wild extravagance would stretch up to 31,680 feet from Point A to Point B. If each of David's steps were approximately 2 feet, 6 paces would be 12 feet. Using the possibility of a full 6 miles, David could have stopped 2,500+ times during the journey, offering 2500+ oxen and the same number of calves. Solomon would later show even greater extravagance bringing the Ark back to this location for the dedication of the Temple (2 Chronicles 5:6).

Now consider zooming 5000 feet toward the clouds for an aerial view of that scene. You would literally see a dotted red stripe leading from Obed Edom's house to David's tent. The earth itself was marked with a blood line.

The image of that thin red thread reminds me of another 2020 dream. Our team was shown a message going out like a red ticker tape. The red tape was a bright thread floating in the air, but soon the scarlet thread became a "text thread" that everyone was either getting or sending.

In this dream, the message written on the thread was simple and direct: "El, my Father, my God – El Elyon – is going to breach the earth soon. The Great Communion Revival."

(Even now as you read, some of you may feel a burning in your heart to text or email a word of encouragement about the Great Communion Revival to your friends and family.)

When you breach something, it means a battle was fought and resistance was overcome. It also means a baby is born, though not without difficulty. A breach baby is the right life in the wrong position. One way or another, God is going to break into our world with new life. Are we in position to receive, to partake, to feast?

But maybe you are asking, why El Elyon? Good question. As the name of God, El Elyon was first mentioned in Genesis 14. After defeating Chedorlaomer and four other kings to rescue his nephew, Lot, we meet a mysterious figure named Melchizedek, who is the king of Salem. And what did Melchizedek do?

He brought out *bread* and *wine*.

> **"And (Melchizedek) blessed him and said,**
> **'Blessed be Abram by *God Most High* (Heb. 'El Elyon'),**
> **Possessor of heaven and earth;**
> **and blessed be *God Most High*,**
> **who has delivered your enemies into your hand!;**
> ***And Abram gave him a tenth of everything.*"** (vv.19-20)

In the coming days of escalating spiritual conflict with the gods of the lands, the motif of Passover and Communion are

The Great Communion Revival

going to increasingly become sources of wisdom and guidance from the Lord, avenues for the release of divine power, with spiritual food to sustain faithfulness. I don't have much to add to the message of this dream except to restate its simple declaration: "El Elyon is going to breach the earth soon. The Great Communion Revival!"

As He does, granting more of Himself, more wisdom, more grace in the bread of His body and the wine of His blood, we will find ourselves not only acting in greater concert with Christ but also operating in true faith as the seed of Abraham and heirs of His promise. A picture of our future is thus prototyped on both sides of the story in Genesis 14.

On the side of prayer, I believe fresh revelation of Christ in His Psalm 110:4 priestly role "according to the order of Melchizedek" will begin to unfold like never before. As we see Him in that light, we will become what we behold. We, His royal priesthood, will increasingly become fitted to the task of intercession with greater and greater ability to bear His burdens. The *ekklesia* will become "Melchizedekean agents" of authority and mercy in equal measure.

On the other side, in the act of Communion (note how priestly bread and wine *triggered* Abraham's tithe) a generation of extraordinary promise will commit in our human enterprise to give Christ, our Great High Priest, the spoils of our labors: a harvest of a tenth of the population of the earth. Call it the Billion Soul Harvest. Call it the last great revival. Call it whatever you want, but it will be massive beyond all imagination.

It will also be contested beyond belief.

chapter 8

THE FINAL BLOOD LINE OF HISTORY

"The blood shall be a sign for you, on the houses where you are. And WHEN I SEE THE BLOOD, I WILL PASS OVER YOU."

Exodus 12:13

The Great Communion Revival

In addition to the two blood lines mentioned in the last chapter, there is a final third: how *the* blood line of Calvary defines our present cosmic conflict. In one way or another, all three point to the great battles of our time and even the end of the age.

Why am I certain a Blood Communion Revival is coming? Simple. Not because of dreams, but because the book of Revelation promises not one, but *two* blood revivals. One is found in Revelation 12, and has to do with saints who overcome by the blood of the Lamb and the word of their testimony. That story redemptively culminates in a wedding feast of rare wine and fine food. I will devote an entire chapter to this matter at the end of this book.

The other story is found in Revelation 17-18.

The former conveys a great move of God leading to the overthrow of the accuser of the brethren. The latter is a drunken, demonic surge of wickedness and immorality led by a harlot called Babylon. This worldwide web of seduction, sorcery, sexuality and malice against the saints is shown to be a *mystery* personified as a *woman* who is a *whore* described as a *city*.

For John to call her Babylon immediately directs the reader to ancient Babel, the originator and epicenter of confusion, division and the occult. Thus she is alluring and seductive in the extreme, but also wanton, brazen and unrepentant. To the degree that you know your values line up with hers yet remain unwilling to change your lifestyle or treatment of others, you are likely under her spell, at least in part. To some degree, the entire world, no less the church, struggles under her influence.[22]

God's anger at Babylon is primarily because she is so successful at seducing His chosen people to desire her delights above His love. Take author Gary Chapman's famous Five Love Languages: 1) Quality time, 2) Words of affirmation, 3) Gifts, 4) Acts of service, and 5) Physical touch, then spend it all on a whore, and you will understand the jealousy of God regarding Babylon! He is a God of limitless love, boundless mercy and infinite beauty and power, while she is a cruel demon. How could we not desire fellowship with Him at every opportunity? It is because she seduces.

In fact, she is a 'dwelling place' for every kind of demon, a petri dish of moral and spiritual bacteria. If you are in her, you are at high risk of profound contamination, yet even knowing this, you may still desire to steal pleasurable moments with her. That is part of her great power. "Wherever there are idolatry, prostitution, self-glorification, self-sufficiency, pride, complacency, reliance on luxury and wealth, avoidance of suffering, violence against life… there is Babylon."[23]

Though her influence is staggeringly vast (Revelation 17:15), any gains made with a prostitute are, by nature, fleeting. A prostitute offers the promise of real connection without real commitment, of intimacy without truthfulness. It is the lie that you can live a lie and somehow not become a liar. By definition, a prostitute will cost you. You *will* pay a price.

As the nexus between political power (kings), economic might (merchants) and false religion (sorcery, mass delusion), Babylon is the defiled mirror image of the Spotless Bride, also called the New Jerusalem. Nevertheless, for the purpose of this book, here's my main point: *Babylon is drunk with the blood of the saints* (Revelation 17:6; 18:24).

The *ekklesia* is given a simple command, "Come out of her," yet in doing so we invite her wrath. Surges in martyrdom will occur as thousands lay down their lives in obedience to the Lamb. The Harlot will drink their blood as if feasting. She *drinks their blood like wine* from a chalice of iniquity (Revelation 17:4,6) and *then makes all the earth drink with her* (Revelation 18:3) as she and the Beast wantonly slay and oppose the saints of God. The picture is of a person in a frenzied state, but the frenzy is a worldwide phenomena. Bloodlust, some might call it, and rightly so.

Do you see that the Harlot offers the world an alternate cup of blood to the cup of Christ? Her appetite is neither quenched nor slaked by the martyr's blood, only fueled by it. This is the unholy revival.

Conversely, at the Last Supper, Jesus promised that Communion would, in a sense, escalate to a time of fulfillment on "that day when I drink it anew with you in My Father's kingdom" (Matthew 26:29, Mark 14:25). In fact, many think Jesus took a Naziritic vow not to physically **"eat it again"** the Communion meal – even in His resurrection – **"until it finds fulfillment in the kingdom of God."** (Luke 22:16). Don't miss this point: the longing of our Lord for full fellowship has a *time of realization*, a period not yet disclosed.

The Removed Veil

Communion, as precursor to the full feast, is a means of contemplation and delight in the joy to come. Communion is a kiss. When a man takes a wife, he lifts her veil so that they can kiss. It anticipates consummation, when they will become one.

Communion is a sort of lifting of the veil. Our shared bread and wine goes far beyond the normal fare of baked flour and fermented juice. It not only assures us that an endless joy is coming, a full feast at high noon when sorrow is no more, but that we can both participate in and help create that future day of celebration, total cleansing of sin, renewal of creation and fullness of hope, in part, today.

The Wedding Feast of the Lamb splendidly and lavishly culminates thousands of years of dreams and promises. Passages like Isaiah 55 **"He who has no money, come!....buy wine and milk...and delight yourself in rich foods"** (vv. 1-2) and also Isaiah 25 are part of this panoply of bridal hope:

> **"On this mountain the LORD of hosts**
> **will make for all peoples**
> a *feast of rich food, a feast of well-aged wine,*
> *of rich food full of marrow,*
> *of aged wine* **well refined.**
> **And He will swallow up on this mountain**
> **the covering that is cast over all peoples,**
> **the veil that is spread over all nations.**
> **He will swallow up death forever."** (vv. 6-8)

But the veil is not only a romantic revelation, it is our final justice. Remember the "end of the Romans Road" dream from chapter three, where Romans 11:12 promises resurrection life for all Christians? This same hope anchors Isaiah 25. The veil over the nations will be removed, not only as that which blinds, but also that which binds. That bondage or wrapping ("the veil over all nations") are the burial clothes of history. We all die. Isaiah 25 promises that those bonds will one day be revoked for good. In the final triumph, death itself will die as God restores us *completely*.

Furthermore, Isaiah said, the reality of that day would be *like a feast of wine and food.*

In another pivotal dream from 2021, Chris Berglund, a covenant friend and our most trusted dreamer, awoke from a deeply impacting dream. Chris dreamt he was inside an historic revival center in California dating back to the 1940s.

In the natural, he had been to this place many times and knew it quite well, but in the dream he was shown a room that few ever visited. A group of folks went with him up some stairs, and then everyone had to climb up a ladder.

(Note: to "climb the stairs" is symbolic of a commitment to the journey to go higher, but to climb a ladder is to connect to Christ. A ladder points to Jesus as the fulfillment of Jacob's dream – the ladder connecting heaven to earth, John 1:51. For this reason it also means that the dream was pointing to receiving a different kind of revelation beyond human means. The dream itself was highlighting not human wisdom, but its own divine strategy).

At the top, many intercessors had now gathered to a special library room. In the dream, Chris noticed a particular book had been placed higher on the shelf than any other book. The title read, *Keys To Praying For The Nations.* Nearby, as if in explanation of the title, a man sat at a desk, transcribing Isaiah 25:6-9 (the very passage I just quoted).

Here's the kicker: in the dream Chris had a deep knowing that the **"feast of rich food…and well-aged wine"** in Isaiah 25:6 referred to the rare privilege of Communion. He knew that to speak of the "best wine" could only point to the wine of Jesus' blood. Similarly, **"the best of meats"** or **"fat things full of marrow"** was indicating the riches of health and wholeness that are released to us in the broken body of Christ.

This is a party, friends. Communion dances on the grave of death. It is a declaration that one day, we shall die no more.

Drawing a Line

Once more, I say, we are in an era shift.

If so, questions abound. Questions, like lines of thought separate one possibility from another. Pray into these and let the Lord speak to you:

Could we be on the cusp of a "higher strategy" (the ladder) reserved for the perils and needs of this generation in the greatest crisis period of human history?

Could a movement of global Communion include whole days spent in spiritual contemplation, feasting together on the body and blood (but also fasting all else *except* bread and wine)?

In such times of focused Communion could the brethren receive from the Lord strategies for breakthrough in the hard, dark places of the earth?

Could nations be ransomed by our intercession?

Could homes begin to shine with light as families celebrate Communion together? Could diseases be healed? Could the Bride's choice for the cup of Christ be part of her exit from Babylon in preparation for His return?

In short, could the biggest revival in human history be connected to the last command Jesus gave before the cross? In

Matthew 26:18, He told His disciples, ***"I will *keep* the Passover,"*** then added, *"Don't forget to do this!* When you do, you are proclaiming something *until I come again."* What if the doing and the proclaiming are more connected to the coming than we have realized?

In either case, Revelation itself promises two blood revivals. One will conclude with the swallowing up of death. The other will demonically delight in causing it. Both movements are thus bathed in blood.

And there it is. There's the line. The Babylonian Harlot will drink her wine. So, too, the Bride will drink hers.

History divides at a line made of blood.

It follows that if the Bride is putting the cup of Christ to her lips with a renewed focus and frequency, then a blood revival among the saints will undoubtedly feature a noticeable increase in our personal and corporate practice of Communion. We will begin to remember the cost of mercy with new gratitude and ponder the price of following the Lamb with new resolve. We will delight with awe and surrender in the tender promise of union with Him. To open to Him, to take Him into us, is to invite His life to overtake ours. And yes, that means we really will fellowship with Him in His suffering.

At a global level, the ramifications are likely staggering. Should we begin to expect a different experience in and from Communion than what our previous church rituals have lacked? If our perspective truly shifted, and the divine meal came to represent degrees of intimate encounter with the Living Christ, warming our soul with revelation and grace as fresh as newly baked bread, then *to feed our spirit in that particular kind of way* – to coordinate meals of sacred bread and divine wine with millions of believers united in that common expectation – would almost certainly *nourish the entire Body of Christ as history has never witnessed.*

Cosmic Conflict

If Passover is our prototype, a Great Communion Revival hints at the protective, overshadowing presence of Christ upon the hearts and homes of millions.

In Goethe's famous work, *Faust*, the title character represents striving, proud ambitious mankind. So blinded by ambition is he that Faust enters into a pact with the devil. The emissary from hell is named Mephistopheles, and requires Faust to sign the pact in blood. At first, Faust regards this as a joke, but Mephistopheles is grave in his reply.

"Blood is a very special fluid," he says.[24]

Christians know (and even sing) the same truth: "There is power, wonder-working power, in the blood of the Lamb!" we say.

But what do we mean? Do we leverage that power in God-ordained ways with biblical insight and intercessory authority? Are we actively protecting, redeeming and preserving a world hellbent on Faustian deals with the devil? If we are a royal priesthood, how do we use the blood of Jesus for Kingdom breakthrough? As a blood rite sanctioned by Christ Himself, could Communion hold a key?

I assure you, the exploding interest in witchcraft, vampirism and shamanism is popularizing experimentation with blood among young people. Pagan religion has no compunction about enticing them to use that power, then seek for more.

By contrast, our understanding of *dunamis* in Jesus' blood has become so formulaic over time – "pleading the blood of Jesus" – that we accidentally risk turning the precious blood of Christ into a sort of Christian magical potion rather than a dynamic, faith-filled, covenantal appeal to our security in Christ.

> **our understanding of "pleading the blood of Jesus" accidentally risks turning the precious blood of Christ into a sort of christian magical potion rather than a dynamic, faith-filled, covenantal appeal to our security in him**

The occult has long recognized the power of blood as a catalytic agent for accessing spiritual energy. Satanic rituals openly rely on the sacred nature of blood to gain dark spiritual power by leveraging the life force of the slain to command evil spirits. One translation of Psalm 59 captures this dynamic when the psalmist prays for protection against "workers of power…men of blood."[25]

Biblically, periods of history-shifting deliverance, such as that of Moses and Jesus (when the deliverer was due), were preceded by government-sanctioned mass murders of children.

Abortion has satanically baptized the nations in a blood ritual of unimaginable evil. From ancient times, pagan cultures practiced human sacrifice as part of their annual feasts or during times of crisis, but never at the scale of our modern plague of government sanctioned infanticide.

Twenty-eight hundred abortions occur globally every 2 hours. By the time you finish reading this chapter roughly one thousand more will have been murdered. As tragic and shocking as that fact is, it barely forms a drop of the innocent blood of babies sacrificed on the altars of legalized abortion. The *Abortion Worldwide Report*, compiled by the Global Life Campaign and released by the Family Research Council in Washington, D.C. on January 25, 2017, revealed the disturbing results of rigorously collected data[26] using publicly available information. The report compiled 100 years of the devastating toll of legalized abortion, beginning with the former U.S.S.R., the first nation to authorize abortion "on demand" in 1920. After examining 100 additional countries where abortion was or has been legal, the report concludes that a staggering *one billion plus babies have been aborted in the last century.*

Read that again. One *billion* human babies. In 100 years.

There is nothing like this. Ever.

Obviously, such a demonic blood ritual must be considered part of the horrible chalice held in the grip of Harlot Babylon, but ancient Babylon is only one of several important historical motifs leveraged by the book of Revelation.

Pick Your Side

More positively, scholars have long seen the typology of Israel's three High Feasts writ large in the text. In particular, Spring's Passover and Autumn's Feast of Tabernacles form bookends by which the Old Testament narrative informs the manner and methods of God's delivering agency at the end of the age. He will mark the saints, judge the gods and rescue His people, then usher them under a canopy of His presence until the days of wrath are complete, after which a golden millennial era will redefine history. Finally, the New Jerusalem will descend, the earth will be cleansed and renewed in a last baptism of fire. And so shall we forever be with the Lord.

We may well be approaching those days, but we are not there yet. If indeed Passover is part of the paradigm, then another trip back to Egypt will help us understand how and why the blood of the lamb so effectively humiliated (and thereby judged) Egypt's power structures, both human and divine. Let's look at what God required of Israel for them to benefit from His protection during the ten plagues.

In ancient Egypt, Amun was the god of the air and one of eight primordial Egyptian deities. His role evolved over the centuries to eventually merge with Ra, the ancient sun god, to become Amun-Ra. Later still, the Greek god, Zeus, would be identified with him. Amun-Ra was considered both the father and protector of Egypt's ruler. Pharaoh was the mortal embodiment of Amun-Ra's divine son.

> "Amon, also spelled Amun, was revered as king of the gods…(and later) identified as Amon-Re. Represented in human form, sometimes with a ram's head, or as a ram…Amon's influence was closely linked to the political well-being of Egypt."[27]

This sheds important light on Exodus 8:22 (echoed also in Genesis 46:34), where Moses argues with God regarding His plan to save the nation.

> "It would not be right to do so; for *the sacrifices that we offer to the LORD our God are an abomination to the Egyptians*. If we offer in the sight of the Egyptians sacrifices that are an abomination to them, will they not stone us?"

Some expositors claim that Egypt despised shepherds because of their lowly social status, or that the statement somehow reflected a common distrust of nomadic peoples by urban dwellers (similar to modern attitudes toward gypsies). Others claim the Egyptians were largely vegetarians (with the possible exception of fish). But to make the claim that the Israelites would be looked at as an "abomination" is unusually strong language if the intent is merely to convey a snooty socio-economic disdain aimed at shepherds by Egypt's wealthy citizenry.

> "This passage suggests that Moses recognizes that the Israelites are going to sacrifice an animal that is sacred to the Egyptians, and that this would be an abomination for the Egyptians. Ostensibly, this is because the ram was the sacred animal of two Egyptian gods, Amun and Khnum.
>
> Amun was a very important god in Ancient Egypt, and in the New Kingdom (1550-1070 B.C.E.) he was seen as the king of the gods, and was syncretized with the sun god as Amun-Ra. It would doubtless have been offensive to the priests of Amun to sacrifice a ram, and there certainly were temples of Amun in the Delta in the vicinity of Goshen and the capital, Pi-Rameses. That

such an act would be offensive would have been clear to any educated person who knew about Egypt in ancient times."[28]

In that light, consider the precise requirement placed upon Israel for their salvation in the Passover. Yahweh was very specific:

> **"You must take a pure unblemished animal, a one year old male from the sheep or the goats. Hold it in safekeeping until the afternoon of *the fourteenth day of the month*."** (Exodus 12:5-6)

Today, the astrological sign of the Ram is called Aries, the name of a Greek god. However, as we have seen, this was the chief token of Amun-Ra, and pharaoh was considered the divine son of Amun-Ra. Is it any coincidence that the sign of the ram is predominant in the month of Nissan, or that it is in the middle of the month, when the moon is full and the predominance of Aries would be at its peak? No, Yahweh chose the precise time to judge the gods of Egypt by placing the sign of His Son on the sacrificial altar for the sake of His people on the fourteenth of the month, exactly when the rule of Egypt's false god and its god-king should have been at their peak power.

To go further, I must turn again to Maimonide's, this time with a direct quote. Born in medieval Spain, Maimonides wrote *The Guide for the Perplexed* in 1190 AD. In that work, he said,

> "Scripture tells us, according to *Targum Onkolos*,[29] that the Egyptians worshipped Aries, and therefore abstained from killing sheep, and held shepherds in

contempt … Some sects among the Sabeans worshipped demons, and imagined that these assumed the form of goats … For this reason those sects abstained from eating goats' flesh. Most idolaters objected to killing cattle, holding this species of animals in great estimation …

In order to eradicate these false principles, the Law commands us to offer sacrifices only of these three kinds (Leviticus 1:2). Thus the very act which is considered by the heathen as the greatest crime, is the means of approaching God, and obtaining His pardon for our sins. In this manner, evil principles, the diseases of the human soul, are cured by other principles which are diametrically opposite.

This is also the reason why we were commanded to kill a lamb on Passover, and to sprinkle the blood thereof outside on the gates. We had to free ourselves of evil doctrines and to proclaim the opposite, viz., that the very act which was then considered as being the cause of death would be the cause of deliverance from death."[30]

Messy Revival

Will such days mark the end of days? In spite of the sovereign protection that rested upon Israel, the social and emotional turmoil caused by the Ten Plagues must have dramatically impacted everyone, not just the Egyptians.[31]

It probably strained the relationships of husbands and wives. The plagues probably frightened and confused many children. Tempers flared. Uncertainty would have been normal.

To bring in a tithe of the earth will be glorious, but *extremely* messy. If a billion souls might truly get swept into the kingdom, how prepared are we for those days? Beloved, none of our present systems are prepared for such a great influx, yet I believe God will do it, nonetheless. More pointedly, I'm not sure any *system* could hold such a harvest anyway, and that's probably by design.

It's going to take a family.

The greater question then becomes a matter of capacity and character, not systems and structure. Is our present depth of conformity to Christ sufficient for the strain of those days? Make no mistake, amidst the intense scoffing and cynicism of our postmodern world, the challenges and human dynamics of mass revival will be profound.

How can people truly love and serve each other when everything in society has primed us for offense and taught us to demand our way? How can the church maintain the meekness and gentleness of Christ in a hostile, "woke" climate, not to mention the sheer numbers of new and very broken believers who will be banging against each other – all of this during the most intense, challenging period of human history?

For this and many other reasons, we must not merely be reactive, we must be proactive. It is time for the church, once and for all, to overcome the accuser of the brethren.

Once again, Communion holds a key.

chapter 9

OVERCOMING THE ACCUSER

*"Before the throne of God above
I have a strong and perfect plea,
A great High Priest whose name is love,
Who ever lives and pleads for me
My name is graven on His hands
My name is written on His heart,
I know that while in heav'n He stands,
NO TONGUE CAN BID ME THENCE DEPART."*

"Before the Throne of God Above"[32]
TRADITIONAL HYMN

The Great Communion Revival

Many scholars consider Revelation 12 the theological heart of the Apostle John's entire vision. As you ponder the message of this chapter, remember that the book of Revelation is not primarily about unmasking the fearful plans of a beastly antichrist, the wicked ways of a harlot called Babylon, or any of the devastating judgments to be unleashed against them. It is primarily the revelation of Jesus.

While the climactic victory of the Lord is assured, the final and complete manifestation of Christ will face greater resistance and rage than any period in human history. Satan will attempt to withstand the Lord, and he will fail. In the end, he will be utterly vanquished. But behind the scenes, John affords a glimpse of the struggle. In the invisible theater of the second heaven, we are told…

> "*Now war arose in heaven,* **Michael and his angels fighting against the dragon. And the dragon and his angels fought back, but he was defeated,** *and there was no longer any place for them in heaven. And the great dragon was thrown down,* **that ancient serpent, who is called the devil and Satan, the deceiver of the whole world – he was thrown down to the earth, and his angels were thrown down with him. And I heard a loud voice in heaven, saying,** '*Now the salvation and the power and the kingdom of our God and the authority of His Christ have come,* **for the** *accuser of our brothers has been thrown down,* **who accuses them day and night before our God.** *And they have conquered him by the blood of the Lamb* **and by** *the word of their testimony,* **for they** *loved not their lives even unto death.*' **(Revelation 12:7-11)**

Allow me to distill a handful of more salient points:

- As stated, Revelation 12 gives us a preview of the full, mythic scope of cosmic war between God and Satan throughout all time, along with how its dramatic conclusion in heavenly realms will transpire at the end of the age. The war pits angelic forces led by the Archangel, Michael, against Satan and his demonic horde.
- Lest the reader mistake its identity, John intentionally connects the dragon to the snake in the garden.
- Furthermore, John identifies the historic cunning and present strategy of Satan in its most cogent form and destructive, successful tactic to be the unceasing work of accusation. In fact, Satan is not the proper name of the archenemy of God, it is his title. In Greek, *Satan* means 'accuser' or, in the legal sense, 'prosecutor.'
- John then implies that the mechanism of accusation is so brilliant that by it Satan has deceived the whole world, including the saints of God. You see, Satan is not just an accuser, *he is a liar who deceives everyone in the way he accuses and in what the accusation produces.*
- One day, Satan will be **"cast down"** or **"thrown down to the earth."** This speaks of the total loss of permission or access to heavenly realms. The overthrowing of Satan *in his accusatory function* will mark the start of the greatest revival ever (**"Now!"** v.10).
- While the battle plays out in heavenly dimensions, it has earthly application. The saints learn to overcome, too. They

do so by **"the blood of the lamb."** In this usage, John is definitely distinguishing between Christ the lamb and Christ the lion (Revelation 5:5, 10:3, 19:11-16). Personality differences between the nature of a powerless, sacrificial lamb and a powerful, predatory lion are meant to be deeply instructive of the mechanism and methods by which the saints will gain victory over Satan in this unique battle.

Outrage Everywhere

In a day when personal rights have become so grossly emphasized, the witness of the Lamb has largely become relegated to our initial salvation experience, but has very little to do with our daily life. When we experience resistance, unfairness or betrayal, our attitude is dangerously aligned more to the sort of entitlement and indignation displayed in the world than by the cross of Christ. While saints are meant to prevail in abundant life, our idea of 'dominion' too often has more in common with stubbornly demanding our way or getting proper payback for wrongs suffered than it does to live out of the inner triumph and contentment of Christ being formed within us.

The world is increasingly polarized about *everything*. Race, education, sexuality, religion, medicine, politics, family, law. We are exhausted in our tribalism, yet more devoted than ever to our tribe and the righteousness of its position. Each side feels they are the proverbial red line of whatever virtue they are committed to defend; they are increasingly the last stand, therefore must increase their stand as a bulwark against the collapse of civilization. Some have called this the "balkanization of culture." We are less and less human as measured by empathy and connection, and more and more neurotic bundles of opinion, outrage and raw nerves, professionals at biting sarcasm and condescending dialogue, perpetually offended with anyone who disagrees. Narcissism has been normalized. It's truly all about me, and the sooner you know that the better we can get along.

It's one thing to see an indictment against the world in those words, it's another thing to see ourselves. But in reality, the Body of Christ is little different from worldly people in our capacity for indignation. Worse, as we feel culture slipping from our grasp into atheism, extreme liberalism and postmodernism with all its inherent anti-Christian sentiment, and with the evaporation of our once pervasive Judeo-Christian ethic, the average Christian is feeling quite squeezed. Our broader place in society is dwindling into loss of respect and loss of historic rights, if not the looming threat of overt persecution.

Author, pastor, and cultural observer, Ed Stetzer, summarized our plight. "Our world, or at least our part of it, seems awash in anger, division, and hostility. Outrage is all around…We find ourselves in an outrage culture…Sometimes it's outrage from Christians, and sometimes it's outrage towards Christians."[33]

Stetzer went on to observe that more and more Christians "are being discipled – literally – by their cable news channel" than by the Word of God. Disciplines of character and grace resulting in the sweet fruit of the Spirit have suffered as a result. Christians are by and large a sour bunch, thank you very much! And with good reason. After all, haven't you noticed, the world is going to hell, and nobody likes us anymore?

But is this the way of the Lamb?

What if all our moral outrage isn't preventing hell from taking over, but rather aiding its advance? If we could see this, maybe we would begin to recognize the truly sinister subtlety and cunning of the serpent's design.

In our unchecked outrage, even should it be over truly outrageous, immoral issues, we are literally feeding the beast.

In fact, this is the exact portrait John paints: what was once a little snake in the garden is now a mighty dragon.

Putting Scripture with Scripture, upon what was that serpent required to feed? The original judgment brought against the snake was to limit its food source to one thing: ***"Dust you shall eat all the days of your life"*** (Genesis 3:14). Even now, it can only eat dust. Does this bring anything else to mind? One chapter earlier in Genesis 2:7, we read, **"the LORD God *formed the man of dust from the ground.*"**

Satan potentially has no source of nourishment outside of what we give him: our emotions, our choices, our actions. The more our personality looks like his, the stronger he becomes. Consider that nothing in the Bible gives us reason to believe the fallen angel called Lucifer is somehow more powerful today than he was in his glorious pre-rebellion state or in his depravity and pride. Yet Revelation 12 shows us that he is now much larger in stature and authority, which begs the question, how? Obviously, for 6000 years, he's been in a feeding frenzy.

By inference we can conclude that the little snake has *been very well fed by humanity*. He has gorged on our agreement with his values and tactics, and grown huge as a result. We have nursed him from a snake of deception slithering through Eden to the global dragon called, "Accuser of the Brethren."

One author ironically pointed out, "The tongue of the adder, visible only briefly, is a small matter."[34] Or so it seems. But it's not.

With our tongue, we give loyalty, nutrition and attention necessary for accusation to thrive. Such is the brilliance of Satan's design, to put so much lethality and poison upon the human tongue. When we claim God's promises, we put God's Word in our mouth. When we accuse, we replace it with Satan's.

To labor in sacrifice and humility is to demonstrate the fruit of the spirit, which directly contradicts the value system of the preeminent overlord of pride. But by cleverly turning all of that energy into accusation against one another, we doubly fool ourselves, feeding Satan while thinking we have attacked him.

> **"So also the tongue is a small member, yet it boasts of great things. How great a forest is set ablaze by such a small fire! And *the tongue is a fire, a world of unrighteousness…*set among our members, staining the whole body, setting on fire the entire course of life, and *set on fire by hell…***
>
> **It is a restless evil, full of deadly poison.** *With it we bless our Lord and Father, and with it we curse people who are made in the likeness of God."* (James 3:5-9)

Admittedly, this gets tricky. Christians are called to be truth-tellers, proclaimers, salt and light. That means challenging corrupt powers in the world around us. We are told to bear witness and be **"the light of the world"** not **"a lamp put under a basket."** (Matthew 5:14-15). We are to stand for righteousness, not bow to idols and lies. Given such high stakes amidst the rising tide of wickedness, it is easy to justify carnal, fleshly attitudes as long as we are fighting for the right thing because the intensity of our methods and emotions can feel like something akin to righteousness.

Nevertheless, our witness is not only positional to truth, it is relational to people. Our message is not only moral, but incarnational. We are to speak the truth in love (Ephesians 4:15), to not only "love in word or talk but in deed and truth" (1 John 3:18). In both instances, our battle has never been with flesh and blood. It must never become so debased and carnal. There is no work of accusation that is not either fleshly or satanic in origin.

The Dilemma of the Right Hand

With this in mind, I now must take three steps back and pose a question that perhaps should have been self-evident, but wasn't.

Given the indications of Scripture regarding the totality of victory achieved by Christ on the cross, how and why is there presently any place in heaven for Satan, therefore any place for 'accusation,' at all?

(Quickly take a minute to read Matthew 12:29; John 12:31-33; Romans 8:37-39, 16:20; Hebrews 2:14; Ephesians 1:20; Colossians 2:14-15 and 1 John 3:8 to get a sense of what I'm talking about).

Psalm 109:6 describes the position of accusation as being at **"the right hand."** In the heavenly trial scene witnessed by Zechariah where Joshua the High Priest was guilty of dereliction of duty, we see **"Satan standing at his right hand to accuse him"** (Zechariah 3:1).

Apparently, when Satan formerly came to present himself to God with accusations against God's people, he would approach the right hand of God's throne. As the symbolic position of God's commitment to justice, Satan could legitimately appeal to God's hatred of sin as a matter of Law, for God would not break His own Law. As prosecutor, Satan was permitted to legally condemn sinners in their sin, which, under the Covenant of Law, invoked curses and punishment upon Abraham's descendants. In Psalm 110:5, God prophetically signaled His plan to upend this system by one day positioning His own Son in that place.

"Sit at my right hand!" God says.

In fact, God so identified with our plight as **"prisoners in misery and chains"** (Psalm 107:10) that by the end of Psalm 109, where the accuser comes to the right hand, He puts Himself **"at the right hand of the needy one, to save him *from those who condemn* his soul to death"** (v. 31).

God chose to become *our* right hand, and thereby determined to upend the legal process that ever permitted a dark rebel power to bring accusation against His beloved children. How would He do this? By positioning the "better blood" of His own Son at the very access point by which condemnation approached the throne in the first place.

Simply stated, in His resurrection, *the priestly blood of Jesus now occupies the seat where accusation once reigned.*

Even though God stated His intentions, no one understood how dramatically He would one day flip the script. Satan could not fathom the willingness of God to die for those whom He loved. He could not comprehend the virtue of the blood that would be shed, or the lamb God would become.

And so it is: the *way* of the lamb – of sacrifice, blood and mercy – is key to defeating him. We can't play an accusation game to defeat the great accuser. We must enter the humility of the cross. He finds it unfathomable. His darkness cannot penetrate that light.

As a result, thanks to the victory of Christ, Satan is now on trial. He has become the principal target of the challenge: **"Who shall bring any charge against God's elect?"** (Romans 8:33). The answer: it is God who *justifies*. Similarly, who is to condemn? Resoundingly, the answer is to be found not only in the blood of Christ, but the position He now occupies.

> **"Christ Jesus is the one who died**
> **– more than that, who was raised –**
> *who is at the right hand of God."* (Romans 8:34)

Because Jesus fulfilled the Law of Moses on our behalf, the new covenant has forever broken Satan's legal right to bring any formal petition or accusation against the redeemed. To us, the Father's throne is eternally a throne of grace. God followed through on His promise to put the mercy of the better blood where accusation once reigned.

Nor was this a temporary fix. Jesus remains *"seated at His right hand"* where? *"in the heavenly places"* (Ephesians 1:20-21). Other verses also attest to this.[35]

So I ask again, in Revelation 12, how is Satan shown to have any access? Has he found a loophole to the blood of Christ? Perhaps, but it's not what you think.

Satan's Deputies?

The blood lacks no efficacy and the cross lacks no totality. Jesus said, **"It is finished"** (John 19:30), and meant it.

Here's the back door for Satan, and likely why his deception is described as being so great as to trick the whole world; why also the saints of God *must* finally become true followers of the Lamb.

The balance of Scripture presents a complicated scenario where Satan's access has truly been removed. His hall pass to the third heaven and God's throne has truly been revoked and he has been displaced in terms of direct permission. But not in indirect. The accusatory role in heaven presently comes from one source: Christians.

How can that be?

First, remember: unbelievers don't have access at all. In salvation, however, God **"raised *US up with Him* and *seated US with Him in the heavenly places* in Christ Jesus"** (Ephesians 2:6).

In this absolutely stunning verse describing the most dramatic reversal in history, the losers finally win. You and I now occupy the position Satan once aspired to, from which he sought to bring condemnation and death. We do so in Christ.

In Christ, *we are seated at God's right hand.*

I have shown in countless passages God's preference for mercy, provision for mercy, and plan for mercy. He closed the "right hand" of Satan's access and opened that door to us instead. He is faithful to us, and will not ever renege on His promise or close that door to us, so if we fall prey to Satan's deceptive schemes and become agents of judgment, then Satan's influence continues. To the degree that *we* bring accusation for him, Satan has access.

Sadly, we do this all the time. Daily. Constantly. In our families, our marriages. Among our friends. Among those with whom we agree and those with whom we disagree. Against that church across the street, or that pastor we don't like so much. Also, against society itself. We speak condemnation and cursing far more than blessings, honor or upliftings. Everyday, Christians bring billions of unsanctified words and thoughts into the throne room. We do so in a spirit of legalism, judgment and Law. We whisper, gossip and divide the Body against itself, then hold the world ransom with our self-righteousness.

satan doesn't need access. he has us!

Beloved, do you see? Satan doesn't need access. By masterfully deputizing God's people to behave no differently than the world, keeping us "wise in our own eyes," and inspiring a constant barrage of decrees and judgments against our brothers and sisters, he's laughing all the way to the bank.

Is it any wonder the world is in the gutter? We never stoop low enough to raise it higher. Our instinct to blame and shame means we rarely practice the art of blessing a stranger, the disruptive joy of forgiving a foe, or the grace to prophecy better things to fallen friends and bitter enemies alike. We don't know how because we ourselves live in the inner swirl of accusation. Every day, Satan lays siege to our minds with a brain-assault that traps us in a desperate cycle of condemnation, ever trying to please God. Under Law-based righteousness, everyone gets flattened by Satan's schemes.

For all these reasons, I believe the nearly impossible task of reversing earth's culture of outrage – **"the blood of the Lamb and the word of their testimony…loving not their lives unto death"** (Revelation 6:9) – is key to the eventual victorious outcome described in Revelation 12. The hinge point of eschatology may be dependent on our humble commitment to embrace the full toll of another's redemption.

The Spirit of the Lamb is to reconcile enemies back into the status of friends. Is it any accident that cancel culture is marked by "unfriending" everyone with whom we disagree?

Perhaps now you can see why I have placed so much emphasis in this book on a deep comprehension of the superior dynamics of new covenant versus old. *We will never overcome the accuser under a system of Law, because Law is precisely the framework by which the accuser is empowered.* Simply put, you cannot be a new creation under the old covenant. You cannot follow the Lamb while sharpening your teeth. You cannot be a minister of reconciliation by adjudicating guilty verdicts upon those who have wronged you.

When we are discipled by the Law of Moses above the Law of Love in Christ, it's hard to even see the problem. Hearts molded by performance, strained by guilt (as the Law requires), will drive us to accuse our brothers and sisters out of a deep sense of inner shame, frustration or insecurity. Deflection is part of the little relief available to us. By favorably measuring ourselves against the sins of others, we convince ourselves we are doing the Lord's work.

We need to get free of this spell. A cosmic struggle against the accuser cannot be won by those who revert to Law-based righteousness. Thus, to overcome by the blood of the Lamb is to fully enter the mystery of Christ. If Satan has leveraged the Body of Christ as skillfully as I have suggested – fractured to the tune of 41,000 denominations around the globe – then we must see how truly broken Christ's body has become. It only makes sense that a different experience, a different embrace of His broken body in sharing Communion together could become the grace we seek: an avenue for personal and corporate healing.

In the Eucharist, my entire orientation becomes radically tenderized to heaven's values. I become humbled as I reconnect with sacrifice. I recenter my righteousness not in anything I can do, only in what He has done. In Communion, each of us becomes confronted with the mission of Christ, beyond our comfort. We are plunged into the call to die to self *("Die before you die. There is no chance after,"* said C.S. Lewis[36]), including the sober realization that the application of mercy to others in their weakness will never be accomplished by demanding our way, only by laying down our lives for them.

Precisely so, as Jesus did, the night He was betrayed.

By a friend.

The Way of the Lamb

To overcome by the blood of the Lamb *and the word of our testimony* is not only to boast in the cross of Christ, but to embrace a lamblike nature. Of that Lamb, Peter says Jesus **"committed no sin,** *neither was deceit found in His mouth. When He was reviled, He did not revile in return;* **when He suffered, He did not threaten, but continued entrusting Himself to Him who judges justly"** (1 Peter 2:22-23).

Who needs release from the prison of your judgment? I'm not talking about whether they are worthy or not, even less about the moral quality of their life choices. I'm talking about the *value of their life before God*. Practically, as Christians, this means we would rather go to the slaughter in silence[37] with blessing and mercy for our enemies, than to bring legal recourse against them, whether for their damnation or our vindication.[38]

Does the LGBTQIA community need your mercy? Drug addicts? Your son? Your wife? Your former business partner? The Democrats? The Republicans? The Russians? The Chinese? The Armenians or Turks or Columbians or…?

In *Longhairs Rising,* I write about the grace to live in this way. A generation is rising, I write,

> "…lion-fierce with love inside, but for that same reason, careful to wear it outside with the gentleness of the Lamb they follow. Biblically speaking, sheep are the species of sacrifice. In a theological sense, that is very nearly their sole purpose. Sheep are defenseless against the knife of the priest. Lambs are even more helpless, the most helpless of sheep.
>
> In Revelation 12:11 we discover the last days strategy by which God creates overcomers: people possessed by sacrificial love. It is *not* the way of the Lamb…
>
> - When we demand our own rights
> - When we clench our fist and slander others
> - When threatened or wronged, we retaliate
> - When we seek our own justice
> - When we use our power to dominate others
>
> While physical martyrdom may be the ultimate realization of our willingness to die for love, there are a thousand lesser martyrdoms of reputation and self that

occur whenever we refuse to perpetuate the cycle of accusation against others. As we release blessing when we are cursed, we operate in the lamblike spirit of Christ.

In the grand, ironic reversal that marks the ways of God, we actually gain authority to roar like a lion when we act like a lamb.

Emulating the lamb is not about being weak enough not to fight but about being strong enough to yield. Yield your will and your rights, even your right to justice, for the sake of a world that needs mercy. But never, never, never yield your heart, your integrity, or your obedience.

The followers of the Lamb that "are coming, wave after wave, are those who will *give their blood, and take none*, until the nations of the earth are won by love. If need be, they will not relent, not even in the face of certain death, until the soil runs red. The Lamb who was slain shall have an army of lambs, who do not fear to die, because they love the Lord, they love the lost, and they 'love not their own lives, even unto death' (Revelation 12:11).

Such raging, unquenchable love forces the reprioritization of our entire lives."[39]

Dietrich Bonhoeffer, the German theologian who was hanged for resisting Hitler, wrote,

"To endure the cross is not a tragedy; it is the suffering which is the fruit of an exclusive allegiance to Jesus Christ. When it comes, it is not an accident, but a necessity. It is not the sort of suffering which is inseparable from this mortal life, but the suffering which is an essential part of the specifically Christian life."[40]

A Dream of the Better Blood

One of the most vivid Communion dreams given to us in the three year period 2020-2022 involved a room full of people who were all waiting with faith for the Great Communion Blood Revival. As we spoke to one another about it, the question came up as to whether we had enough 'BB' diplomas to hand out for the Communion service that would occur later that night. In the dream, one of the women in the room answered, "Every time one is handed out, they multiply."

"After this, the scene changed. We were all watching a wall-sized live interactive map of the U.S. where homes, streets and highways would light up as people began partaking of Communion and receiving these diplomas. I (the dreamer) watched an interactive live map titled the Trail of Death. As individuals and groups received Communion, the map would light up with blue and red lights so that the lights accentuated the map.

At the same time, a great darkness rose up across the country as universities, colleges, schools, homes, and witch covens partook of a different kind of Communion service. Their Communion was perverse: a toxic cocktail of anger, accusation, unforgiveness and blood. They too were handing out diplomas, called 'BA,' and the BAs were also multiplying.

I knew that BB diplomas stood for "Better Blood" while BA stood for "Brethren Accusers." Both had power and both were warring against one another. Yet, only the BB had true authority.

Our team began talking about how we can't fight power with power, we needed to fight power with authority. Somebody began quoting Luke 10, saying "The authority we have been given over all the power of the enemy is through the Better Blood…"

<u>if the world knows us more by our constant moral superiority than our beautiful mercy, we have not yet become students of the better blood</u>

Graduation speaks of the culmination of training and enculturation. Indeed, as the earth graduates to the Kingdom age, the wheat and the tares are about to be fully revealed for the paths they have chosen. I want to practice our *common union*, to consume the Lamb and *become* a lamb, in such a way that I forever weaken the accuser of the brethren to the degree that I am able. I want to decommission my deputy badge. For too long, Satan has deployed billions of members of the Body of Christ to serve as co-prosecutors against one another, and against a fallen world.

Fine, you say, "but I'm not going to let people just walk all over me!" But what if that's what it takes to break this cycle?

Jesus said, **"I am sending you out as lambs in the midst of wolves"** (Luke 10:3).

Newsflash: *wolves aren't supposed to be afraid of sheep*. Sheep are bait. Sheep are attractive to wolves. Sheep are dinner.

What if the person looking for a fight finds you turning the other cheek instead? What if they steal from you, and rather than sue them into tomorrow, you give more besides? How have we come to believe that we can win the world by arming ourselves to the teeth in the culture wars? In Matthew 5, Jesus taught an entirely different set of values.

> **"Blessed are those persecuted for righteousness' sake...Blessed are you when others revile you and persecute you and utter all kinds of evil against you falsely on my account...Blessed are the peacemakers, for they shall be called the sons of God."** (vs. 9-11)

Disciple, do you want to be *like* the Son of God?

> **"He was oppressed, and He was afflicted,**
> *yet He opened not his mouth;*
> *like a lamb that is led to the slaughter,*
> **and like a sheep that before its shearers is silent,**
> so *He opened not His mouth."* (Isaiah 53:7)

No teeth. No raging chatter in the comment box. Just suffering, enduring, on behalf of another. Because God has done the same for you, you are invited to be like Him.

If the world knows us more by our constant moral superiority than our beautiful mercy, we have not yet become students of the better blood.

The Great Communion Revival

NOTES & REFLECTIONS

EXCURSUS C
"Experience of Divine Love"

In her essay[41] exploring Julian of Norwich's experience of God's divine love, culminating in a mystical revelation of the utter importance of Jesus' blood, author Marisa J. Lapish writes:

"Julian's view of time is encapsulated in her word of choice—poynte. As she focused on the cross, Julian experienced a concentrated view of God which is instantaneous where all people and 'all manner of thing' are layered prism-like, situating and defining every space and every moment of time in that place of divine love expressed through his blood…

Her visions are full of healing imagery, where the 'blessed Trinity will make well all things which are not well,' unveiling the shalomic kingdom redemption of restorative love and salvific theosis. Jesus' blood therapeutically and kenotically heals, without wrath, without shame, and without blame, but with mercy, with compassion, and with deep love. The wounds of humanity are healed by Jesus' own bloody wounds. This means that the wounds that others have inflicted and the wounds that I have caused are being held and being healed in the blood that flows from divine love. All are welcome to this iconic Eucharistic table for who, in all of humanity, could possibly be excluded from the love of Jesus?

The Eucharist invites us to enter into the reality of the kingdom of divine love, to be people whose identity is wrapped up in self-

giving...to become 'broken bread and poured-out wine' in a world of suffering and bloody messes...

Just imagine how we might eat that way in our churches! No denominational, doctrinal or baptismal lines formed or drawn to receive the Eucharist. No proof of holiness or purity certificates required to eat bread and drink wine at the family table where everyone hungers and thirsts and is fed with divine righteousness and sustained by divine love with generous, open-hearted hospitality. All are welcome to this Eucharistic preview of the festal banquet of kingdom shalom because Jesus is present with His suffering ones and Jesus is present in the faces we see across the table, His iconic wounded children.

Just imagine how we might eat sacramentally in our homes, through ordinary liturgy of a shared meal with people not typically on our guest list! Might bread and fish multiply with abundance if we shared our littleness, our hazelnuts, with neighbors in eucharisteo, giving thanks? After hours of talking about Jesus along our neighborhood Emmaus roads, might strangers in our community invite us to their dinner tables and finally recognize Jesus when we break bread together in their safe abodes? In our shared experience of woundedness and suffering, might we lean into the story in another's heart with solidarity, listening and lingering over glass of wine or a cup of coffee? Might we defy isolation and pessimism by holding each other closely to recognize Jesus' loving presence in the midst of us and within us in the reality of our bloody messes and the heartbreak of our collective community trauma?

---

chapter 10

THE DIVINE MEAL

*"I was made by you, I was made for you,
I am unfulfilled without FULL COMMUNION."*

"Since Your Love"[42]
CONTEMPORARY WORSHIP SONG

The Great Communion Revival

As we approach the end of this book, I remind the reader of a statement I made in the beginning. If God could be said to have a dream, some longing that must necessarily manifest in time and space, we should expect to see His dream spelled out in Scripture. And so we do. From start to finish, God's desire is to have a people who will love Him as much as He loves them, and to fellowship with that people in unfettered, unbroken joy.

One of the most intimate ways we could describe such fellowship is with a word: Communion. To to commune with God is to *come into union.*

It is no accident that communion of this sort comes in the form of a meal. Being made in the image of God, humans find greater, more consistent delight – soul-satisfying brotherhood, sisterhood and friendship – in a shared meal than almost any other human endeavor. Meals offer laughter, memory and sensory delights. Meals create shared experiences. In every culture and over all periods of time, people have bonded over good food.

The late American poet, Maya Angelou, said that "when you invite someone to sit at your table and you want to cook for them, you're inviting a person into your life."

Cesar Chavez famously observed, "If you really want to make a friend, go to someone's house and eat with him…The people who give you their food give you their heart."

What does it mean to share a meal where someone gives you their heart? Aspects of God relating to humans in this manner can be seen in various instances comparing many of His blessings to food and meals. The many delights of the Promised Land (Deuteronomy 8:7-10, 26:9) and the riches of the Word of God are frequently compared to food (Psalm 19:10; Jeremiah 15:16; Ezekiel 3:1-2). Extending this thought, fellowship with God is similarly compared to the sweetness, sustenance or nourishment of food. Jesus said His "food" was to do the will of God (John 4:34). We are told in Psalm 34:8 to, **"Taste and see that the Lord is good,"** while Psalm 36:8 tells us God will help us to "feast on the abundance of (Your) house, and You give them drink from the river of Your delights."

So not only does God provide our natural sustenance in food and drink (as creation was designed to do, see Genesis 1:29), but *God Himself is food and drink.*

In John 6:35, Jesus declared that He alone was the true **"bread of life."** As if to underline that point, Jesus was born in Bethlehem, which means, "The House of Bread." So if the two main components of Communion are bread and wine, surely we are meant to see that Jesus is offering so much more than bread and wine. Whether you are Catholic or Protestant, Communion is a divine meal by which Jesus shares with us His heart. How will *you* eat such a meal?

Typically people eat because they are hungry. In the space between meals, we begin to feel *empty* and want to feel *full* instead. But if God is Spirit (John 4:24), how do we feed on Him, and if God is invisible, where do we go to get full?

Psalm 16:11 points us in the proper direction: *"**In Your presence** there is **fullness** of joy."*

Manna and the Bread of Presence

God miraculously sustained Israel in the wilderness for forty years on manna, called the bread of heaven. The mystery of manna has never been seen before or since, yet Jesus declared in that manna was hidden a picture of how God wanted to feed humanity with Himself (John 6:33).

In the construction of the Tabernacle only a few ordained implements were included in the blueprint. Inside the Holy Place, which is a picture of man's soul, there were three items: a seven-branched Candlestick for illumination (representing the light of revelation and truth), an Altar for incense (representing prayer and intercession), and a Table filled with daily, fresh bread (representing the sustaining of life in food and fellowship).

This bread, the "Bread of the (Divine) Presence" was also called "showbread." It consisted of twelve loaves placed on the table every Sabbath and replaced a week later, at which time the old loaves would be eaten by the priests as part of their provision. Interestingly, the design of a sacred Table with bread has corollaries in other Ancient Near Eastern cultic rituals, but with clear and important distinctions in Israel's implementation. In pagan thought, the gifts of food were presented behind the veil, supposedly in the direct presence of the deity, and given for the deity's nourishment. Israel models but corrects this critical error.

As directed by Yahweh, the Table is in the antechamber, the Holy Place, separated from the Holy of Holies by the curtain, rather than contained within it (Exodus 26.31-35).

> "This partition between God and the Table makes it clear that the bread of display is not actually consumed by God but is only a token gift--this is also underlined by the fact that it was eaten by priests...the furnishings and acts of devotion performed upon them all belong to the

outer sanctum, and the partition dividing the two realms is never breached. Thus God, even as His presence dwells among the Israelites, is perceived as separate from them and noncorporeal."[43]

Holy and all-powerful, God does not need human bread. He does not "need" anything. Nevertheless, by viewing the design of the Tabernacle as a type of humanity (Outer Court as body, Holy Place as soul, and Holy of Holies as spirit) we can see how God brilliantly flipped the pagan idea of feeding God by commanding that bread blessed by His presence would become *food for the priesthood* instead.

If nearness to God was the high privilege of the Levitical priesthood, bread became its physical embodiment. Such bread was communal, representational and holy. With twelve loaves standing for the twelve tribes, God kept Israel freshly before Him, a relationship which the priesthood mediated by making the concern and care of such things a part of their daily rhythm.

<u>the desired association becomes plain: though invisible, God is present in the bread. He alone is our true source of life. if true for the Levitical priests, how much more for the royal priesthood of the new covenant?</u>

The desired association becomes plain: though invisible, *God is present in the bread.* He alone is our true source of life. If true for the Levitical priests, how much more for the royal priesthood of the new covenant?

The Bread of the Presence shows how God wants to proverbially dine with us and know us, and we, Him. This longing is beautifully portrayed in the words Jesus spoke at the Last Supper.

Sharing a Meal with God

> **"When the hour came, (Jesus) reclined at table, and the apostles with Him. And He said to them, *'I have earnestly desired to eat this Passover with you* before I suffer.'"** (Luke 22:14-15)

Wait a second, what is Jesus saying? After all, they've eaten a ton of meals together, including at least two previous Passovers. True, but they haven't eaten *this* meal. Apparently, this is a different kind of Passover. Listen to the longing in the words of Christ.

"I have *earnestly desired.* To eat. *With* you."

In that simple, short phrase we discover thousands of years of divine desire. Here it is, the dream of God: fellowship restored. God is a romantic! His divine yearning shall never be quenched or diminished.

> **"Love is strong as death, jealousy is fierce as the grave.**
> **Its flashes are flashes of fire, the very flame of the LORD.**
> **Many waters cannot quench love."** (Song 8:6-7a)

While the day of consummation lies yet ahead, Jesus institutes a simple, sacred process by which we can enjoy measures of intimacy and joy along the way, in the delight of one another's company, and in the satisfaction of being present with one another. In Christ, Passover becomes the shared meal of our deliverance and redemption, but *this* Passover was unique. Jesus is hinting at a long period of anticipation, almost as if the Godhead has been holding their breath.

I put before you, the Last Supper was, for Jesus, a return in the memory of God to the power, thunder and lightning of Sinai.

> **"Then Moses and Aaron, Nadab, and Abihu, and seventy of the elders of Israel went up, and *they saw the God of Israel*. There was under His feet as it were a pavement of sapphire stone, like the very heaven for clearness. And He did not lay His hand on the chief men of the people of Israel; *they beheld God, and ate and drank.*"** (Exodus 24:9-11)

There on the mountain, seventy four men ascend to formally ratify a covenant of works and Law. In His omniscience, of course, God knew that man would not and could not fulfill the promises of obedience the nation had made...Regardless, Law would now bind them to obedience, resulting in blessing or curses. So a meal was prepared, but the meal was incomplete.

Note: *they* ate.

God did not.

This was not truly fellowship, for the Law affords nothing of the sort. As evidence of that painful fact, God refrained from the meal. He did not eat because such a meal was not yet the realization of His dream. Instead, He waited, revealing Himself progressively, more and more, in covenant faithfulness, patience and mercy, in patterns, shadows and types, until everything culminated in the historical fact of God becoming Man so that He could finally establish a new covenant by which true fellowship with God was possible once more.

True communion deserves a true meal.

This is the covenant meal both parties can enjoy, for God is literally present not only at the meal, but in the meal. Emmanuel, God With Us, present in the glorious fire at Sinai, could not there eat, but now He can.

Do you see now. Jesus said, "Boys, you have no idea how long I've waited, or how earnestly I've desired *this* meal."

At the first covenant meal, rules were written in stone, but in the sacrifice of His own life, Jesus is preparing to write them in the softened flesh of regenerated human hearts. Yes, the Son of God has looked forward to this meal for a long, long time.

Let this strike you to your core. What He could not yet provide under the terms of Sinai, He now offers freely in the covenant of grace: the ultimate food of life, Himself. Will you view it with equal parts reverence and joy as the expectation of a friend knocking on your door, eager to sup with you? Or will it be like a rushed, bland fast food drive-thru because you don't have time for anything else? History is, in a sense, the process by which God has given humanity time to choose on what they will feed, with whom they shall spend their time, and from what source they shall find their greatest possible delights.

Said Richard J. Foster, "We who have turned our lives over to Christ need to know how very much He longs to eat with us, to commune with us. He desires a perpetual Eucharistic feast in the inner sanctuary of the heart."[44]

And though not specifically addressing the Eucharist, Dallas Willard nonetheless offers insight into the potential of the sacred encounter when he writes,

> "In the union and communion of the believer with God, their two beings (become) unified and inhabit each other, just as Jesus prayed: 'that they may all be one' ... As we grow in grace, God's laws increasingly form the foundation of our hearts, his love is our love, his faith our faith."[45]

By paraphrasing Saint Augustine, I believe most of the point/counterpoint can be nipped in the bud with a simple, inarguable dichotomy. "We do not sin when we adore Christ in the Eucharist; we do sin when we do *not* adore Christ in the Eucharist."[46]

A Bloodless Faith?

There is no way around the graphic nature of Communion. If a preacher were to say about himself what Jesus said, it would make us squirm uncomfortably. We seem to want a bloodless faith that risks no offense and conveys nothing that would make our rational minds squeamish. *Sola Scriptura*, the great cry of the reformers, can nonetheless seem quite selective at times. Scripture alone…when it suits us.

When the Second Temple was destroyed in Jerusalem in 70 AD, Judaism became a sacrificial religion without blood sacrifices. Due to the lack of a physical Temple (the only authorized location for ritual sacrifice), therefore nothing for the Levitical priesthood to do, and having no Day of Atonement, how would Israel remain distinct among the nations? Rabbinic Judaism began spiritualizing sacrifice in distinctive ways and physicalizing other rituals to substitute for the act of sacrifice. For example, the blood of circumcision took on greater significance as a covenantal ritual.

Jesus, knowing that the ultimate Temple of His Body was going to be torn down, implemented the act of Communion for similar reasons. Christians understand that the sacrificial system has found its highest achievement in the work of Christ, but that, too, makes Christianity a sacrificial religion without blood sacrifice.

Or is it? Listen to what Jesus said. We allegorize, but the words of Jesus are quite red and quite blunt. It's hard to reduce these words to pure symbolism.

> **"I (Jesus) am the living bread that came down from heaven. If anyone eats of this bread, he will live forever . . . the bread that I will give for the life of the world is My flesh. For *My flesh is true food, and My blood is true drink. Whoever feeds on My flesh and drinks My blood abides in me, and I in him* . . . This is the bread that came down from heaven, not like the bread the fathers ate, and died. Whoever feeds on this bread will live forever."** (John 6:51, 55-56, 58)

Do those words confuse or upset you? If so, you are in good company.

> **"When many of His disciples heard it, they said, 'This is a hard saying; who can listen to it?' But Jesus, knowing in Himself that His disciples were grumbling about this, said to them, *Do you take offense at this?...It is the Spirit who gives life; the flesh is no help at all. The words that I have spoken to you are spirit and life.*"** (John 6:60-63)

Our Evangelical and charismatic churches tend to water this down, even though Jesus said His words are spirit and life. He said, of Himself, that the bread of Christ's body and the wine of His blood should be considered *true* food and *true* drink. I don't want watered down truth.

Ironically, the very ritual that is supposed to unite and endear the members of Christ's body to one another has become one of our most divisive and bitter points of contention. Rather than binding ourselves together in the remembrance of the cross, the material and theological substance of Communion critically divide us. Surely heaven must view this as a tragedy beyond fathoming.

Simply stated, the question has largely divided into two camps: is Communion a feast *upon* God, or is it merely a beautiful symbol of His great sacrifice? In 1215, in the Fourth Council of the Lateran, the Roman Catholic Church decreed that in the doctrine of transubstantiation the Eucharist *literally* became the body and blood of Christ, while later Protestants typically saw it as symbolic, though by degrees.

The Great Communion Revival

Both Lutherans and Catholics affirm that, in the Eucharist, Christ is "present wholly and entirely, in His body and blood, under the signs of bread and wine"[47] though Catholics believe the body and blood of Christ literally, physically manifest in the elements, while Lutherans believe the presence of Christ is literal, while remaining primarily spiritual. In either event, it would seem the Eucharist is more than a mere commemoration or symbol.

Note the spirit, character and directness with which the early church fathers spoke of the experience of Communion for themselves. Remember, too, that many of these were directly discipled by one of twelve apostles. Others could be cited, but this handful will suffice to demonstrate how important Communion was to them.

- Shortly after 100 A.D., in his *Letter to the Romans 7:3*, Ignatius of Antioch, a disciple and co-worker with the Apostle John, said, "I have no taste for corruptible food nor for the pleasures of this life. I desire the Bread of God, *which is the flesh of Jesus Christ*, who was of the seed of David; and for drink *I desire His blood*, which is love incorruptible."[48]

- In his work, *Against Heresies 4:18:4-5*, Irenaeus of Lyons (c. 140-202 A.D.) said *"the new sacrifice of the new covenant"* embodied not just the two elements of bread and wine, but in them "the earthly and heavenly."

- Tertullian (c. 155-250 A.D.) wrote, "The flesh feeds on *the body and blood of Christ*, so that the soul too may fatten on God" *(Resurrection of the Dead 8:3)*.

- Lastly, around 150 A.D, Justin Martyr (who was likely instructed by John's disciples in Ephesus) explained the depth of the presence of Christ in the divine meal. In a defense of Christianity written to Emperor Antoninus Pius, Justin wrote, "We call this food Eucharist; and no one is permitted to partake of it, except one who believes our teaching to be true...*For not as common bread nor common drink do we receive these*; but...as we have been taught, *the food which has been made into the Eucharist...is both the Flesh and the Blood of that incarnated Jesus.*"[49]

From Lord's Supper to Lord's Prayer

Is there a connection between these two? As central as both were in the teachings of Jesus, it would seem likely. A dream helped point us in the right direction. In early 2022, Chris Berglund awoke from a deeply impacting dream. In the encounter...

"A voice declared, 'I Am is preparing to answer the Disciples' Prayer worldwide: The Great Communion Prayer!' After that statement, Chris found himself in a massive theater with a choir somehow positioned between heaven and earth singing the most glorious rendition of *The Lord's Prayer*. In the dream, the voice continued to speak.

'Envelope this with two witnesses!'

Another voice added, 'Make it John 17 and Psalm 23.'

To which the main voice simply replied, 'Good.'"

Chris then saw the words of the Lord's Prayer floating in the air. John 17 and Psalm 23 began floating in the air along with the prayer, wrapping around it, enfolding it.

I find this dream fascinating on multiple levels. First, the Lord's Prayer has always been a bit misnamed, since the words we recite are the result of the disciples asking Jesus to teach *them* how to pray. It wasn't the prayer of Jesus, it was a training tool. A more accurate name would be the Disciples' Prayer.

The very middle of the Disciples' Prayer teaches us to pray this: "Give us this day our *daily bread* and *forgive us* our trespasses."

Daily bread. With forgiveness of sins. Sound like anything?

> **Could daily bread and forgiveness point to a theological and experiential fusion of Communion embedded in the Disciple's Prayer? Is that portion of the Disciples' Prayer a sort of portable Communion?**

Could daily bread and forgiveness point to a theological and experiential fusion of Communion embedded in the Disciples' Prayer? Could it be a verbal recitation by which that portion of the prayer was designed by the Lord to help all of us remember, meditate upon, and proclaim the act of Communion, with or without bread and wine at our disposal? Is that portion of the Disciples' Prayer a sort of portable Communion?

Bread for His broken body. Wine for forgiveness of sins.

And so we pray: "Give us this day our daily sustenance of deep communion with You. Let us feed on Your sacrifice, experience Your healing life, and savor the wine of mercy."

According to the dream, we should surround the Lord's Prayer with meditations on John 17 and Psalm 23. The depths of communion expressed in John 17 convey the riches of divine fellowship for which humanity is intended, and destined, and the Trinity's satisfaction with that plan. From such love, from Father to Son, from God to us, from us to God, and from us to one another, the greatest revival in history is promised: "the world" will believe in the mission of Jesus.

> "*...that they may all be one, just as You, Father, are in Me, and I in You,* **that they also may be in Us, so** *that the world may believe* **that You have sent Me…I in them and You in Me, that they may become perfectly one, so** *that the world may know that You sent Me and loved them* **even as You loved Me….**
>
> **I made known to them Your name, and I will continue to make it known, that** *the love with which You have loved Me may be in them, and I in them.*" (John 17:20-23, 26)

Similarly, Chris recalled how the Lord had previously impressed upon him the importance of Psalm 23. When the Lord reminded him of the "table in the midst of your enemies" he asked the Lord to show him that table. To his surprise, he was shown a Communion table.

Over and over we see the possibility of the divine meal embedded in places we have not thought to look. But for now we must turn attention from the bread to the wine.

Four Cups

Solomon long ago gave instruction we would be wise to apply directly to Communion, "**Eat your *bread* with joy, and drink your *wine* with a *merry heart*** " (Ecclesiastes 9:7).

While this entire book might seem quite sober in its focus, more often than not Communion should be joyous in its reality. It's not drudgery, it's delight! Don't just limit it to crackers and juice. Instead, make it part of a feast. *Celebrate* Communion, don't just perform it.

We often forget that Jesus (along with all of Israel) was literally reenacting The Passover when He ate the meal with His friends. To this day, Passover is the preeminent tradition of Jewish identity because it is the preeminent event of Jewish history. While some portions of the ceremony evolved over time, our tendency to think of a single cup of wine is likely in error. The tradition of four cups has been present since at least the first century A.D. and was likely a part of the Last Supper.

The inspiration behind the tradition of four cups varies. Most agree, however, that the tradition is based on the four "I Wills" of Exodus 6:6-7:

> "**Say, therefore, to the sons of Israel, 'I am the LORD, and I *will* bring you out from under the burdens of the Egyptians, and I *will* deliver you from their bondage. I *will* also redeem you with an outstretched**

arm and with great judgments. Then I *will* take you for My people, and I will be your God; and you shall know that I am the LORD your God, who brought you out from under the burdens of the Egyptians.'"

The four cups are called by different names because it is difficult to encapsulate the full meaning with one English word, yet the full picture is meant to harmonize the scope of the four promises God spoke.

- The Cup of Sanctification: "I will bring you out"
- The Cup of Deliverance/Judgment: "I will deliver you"
- The Cup of Redemption/Blessing: "I will redeem you"
- The Cup of Praise/Hope/Kingdom/Restoration: "I will take you for My people"

From a Jewish perspective, the First Cup of Sanctification ("I will bring you out") doesn't sanctify the person, it sanctifies the *night*. It does not make the celebrants holy or separate but rather sets aside this night as truly special, "different from all other nights" of the year. In fact, none of the meanings of the Four Cups can be properly derived apart from the memory and purpose of the main event, the first Passover.

The Second Cup ("I will deliver you") comes much later. After reading Psalm 113-114, participants are encouraged to boast in Yahweh for what He has accomplished through the Passover, signifying the mighty acts of Yahweh in judgment on the gods of Egypt.

The Third Cup ("I will redeem you") follows the meal *and* the breaking of bread (called the *'afikomen')*. Note the timing of the cup. In each of the gospels, it is only after the breaking of the bread that Jesus defines His actions as an enactment of Passover while redefining it as a new covenant to be accomplished by Himself as the new Isaac, the firstborn of God, and the sacrificial lamb. If tradition holds, since each account agrees, Jesus likely raised the third cup: the Cup of Redemption.

"Drink all of it! I'm making a *new* covenant!"

With that statement Jesus directly and incredibly sanctifies Communion as an event of paramount importance, comparable only to the one that took place 1,400 years before His birth, while also surpassing it in scope and glory. The average Christian may read the events of the Last Supper and merely see the institution of a new "Christian" event, a sacrament memorialized in ritual, but it was (and is) so much more. Jesus equated His own blood with that of the Paschal lamb. He was both reenacting, incarnating and self-animating the entire panoply of Passover's history and significance. He was identifying Himself, that night, that action, and *that* CUP, as the culmination and connection of centuries of tradition, prophecy, and hope.

In so doing, He also linked the Cup of Redemption to Jeremiah's 600-year old prophecy which gives four new "I wills."

"I *will* make a new covenant...not like the covenant that I made with their fathers on the day when I took them by the hand to bring them out of the land of Egypt...I *will* be their God, and they shall be My

people...for I *will* forgive their iniquity, and I *will* remember their sin no more." (Jeremiah 31:31-34)

The "I will redeem" promise of the Passover, boldly exegeted by Jeremiah's prophecy 600 years prior, was tenderly enfleshed by Christ as He raised the Third Cup and announced that He was about to culminate *all* of redemptive history – from Passover, judging the gods of Egypt, breaking the power of slavery, demonstration of God's covenant love and power to save His people, and the blood of the Lamb at the center of it all – to the enactment of a new covenant with God that extended that narrative from the garden to the Upper Room, and a cup of wine held in the hands of the Son of God, who was about to become the Lamb Who Was Slain.

One last cup remains, and this is likely the cup that Jesus foreswore until He could drink it eternally. In essence, He undertook a Naziritic vow which He has sustained for 2000 years, waiting until we could share that cup together with Him at the feasting table when He adorns Himself as Bridegroom and we enter His glory and fullness as the cosmic Bride. Believers have been made "accepted in the beloved" and Peter declares that we are to **"proclaim the excellencies of Him who called you out of darkness into His marvelous light. Once you were not a people, but now you are God's people"** (1 Peter 2:9-10).

Could Jesus have intended the "daily bread" of the Disciples' Prayer, along with its daily appeal for forgiveness, as pointing to a far more frequent Communion habit? Again, by embedding key aspects of Communion into the form of a prayer, are we meant to essentially "pray our Eucharist" with full Christ-awareness even when no bread or wine is available? Is the remembrance Jesus intended not because He assumed we would do it sparsely, but rather because He desired to rhythmically sear His own vibrant memory and loving sacrifice upon our wandering devotion, thus making His presence a constant North Star for our affections.

In short, was the early church committed to Communion beyond a rote and occasional ritual? A closer look will show the idea is not so far-fetched.

"Breaking Bread" in the Early Church

Frederick Buechner once explained that there are two ways of remembering. One way is to make an excursion from the living present back into the dead past" and the other way is to summon the past "back into the living present." He added, "When Jesus said, 'Do this in remembrance of Me,' He was not prescribing a periodic slug of nostalgia."[50]

Several New Testament passages point to the early church frequently sharing a common meal (Luke 24:35, Acts 2:42, 46 and 1 Corinthians 10:16), but was the meal they shared simply lunch or dinner? Doubtful. The language is too specific. If it were a common meal, Scripture could simply say "they ate together" or "shared a meal." Instead, it says they **"broke bread."** These references likely point to an early church practice we've lost, namely the frequent sharing of the Lord's Supper.

Consider how repeatedly we read that they **"broke bread"** together. On their final day in Troas, the night before Paul departed, Luke says in Acts 20:7 that they all **"were gathered together to break bread."** Mind you, no one is certain if they will see Paul again. It's a serious occasion.

"Breaking bread" has instead become a colloquialism for sincere and warm-hearted fellowship. Don't get me wrong, fellowship is definitely good. Meals together are spiritual and enriching and Communion should be both. I believe we should share more life around a table of food, not less. But this begs the question, if a common meal holds spiritual riches, why not add to the richness with a true spiritual feast? Why not begin or end *all* our meals together with family or friends (or at least many more than we presently do) with the elements of Communion, and time for remembrance?

After His resurrection, when Jesus sat with some of His disciples on the famous road to Emmaus in Luke 24:13-35, He took bread and "broke it." Once again, Scripture employs that specific phrase. Was it just a meal? Probably not. Later, these same disciples told the apostles how Jesus was revealed to them *in the breaking of the bread* (Luke 24:35).

1 Corinthians 10:16 connects Communion – the breaking of bread and the Lord's Table (v. 21) – into one thought unit. Letting Scripture interpret Scripture, the phrase "breaking bread" is thus likely a figure of speech called a *synecdoche* where a "part stands for the whole." In other words, "breaking bread" is not simply fellowship at a meal, but points to a particular experience. The phrase is too evocative to merely be sentimental.

The full continuum of salvation and redemption stretches from Passover to the Passion, and somehow all of it is packed into a meal we rarely enjoy. When we do, we treat it as purely symbolic and nothing else. But what if aspects of Jesus still await our discovery in the breaking of the bread? What are we missing by our "take it or leave it" approach to Communion, by subsisting on

The Great Communion Revival

a thin "once a month" diet of a dry little cracker or tasteless starch wafer with thirty pre-prepackaged drops of watered-down grape juice, barely enough to wet the tongue?

Notice in Acts 2:42 the spiritual nature of every listed item: doctrine (1 Timothy 1:3), fellowship (1 John 1:3-7), breaking bread (Acts 20:7), and prayers (Acts 12:5). Notice also that the Greek uses a definite article – "the" – so that the phrase reads, **"the breaking of *the* bread."** Not just any bread, but specific bread broken in a specific way and consumed for a specific purpose. This is clearly unleavened bread and the fruit of the vine. This is the **"Lord's Supper"** (1 Corinthians 11:20), the **"Lord's Table"** (1 Corinthians 10:21), and **"Communion"** (1 Corinthians 10:16).

Three centuries later, the practice had hardly diminished. Prior to the formation of the Roman Catholic Church, in the *Letter of Basil to a Patrician Lady Caesaria,* St. Basil the Great (c. 330-379 A.D.) spoke of taking Communion four times a week, plus as often as other special occasions required.

As we can see, the experience of Communion was likely far more common, therefore far more important, than we have typically understood. The routine and diligence with which the early disciples gave themselves to the discipline of Communion may in fact be part and parcel of the abiding presence of God that marked the book of Acts.

SECTION TAKEAWAYS

1. Blood is not only theology, it is a reality of life. Bloodlines divide cosmic history, while appearances of blood in Scripture are almost always meant to signal the reader that a particular story in some way points to Christ.

2. The diverse and beautiful usage of bread in the Old Testament, both in the form of manna and the Bread of the Presence, are meant to deepen our understanding of the fellowship God desires in Communion. The wine and bread are more than symbolic. They are true manifestations of God's gracious presence with us.

3. Until we understand the way of the Lamb, we will likely continue to be victims of the accuser of the brethren. Even worse, we may be responsible for sustaining him when the clear intent of God is to see him utterly cast down. We must first cast him down in our own hearts (and mouths) if we want to see the full triumph of Christ on the earth. Communion is a means not only to enhance this transformative inner work, but to also reenact the triumph of Christ with spiritual and cosmic iconography.

NOTES & REFLECTIONS

The
LAMB WAVE

chapter 11

THE
LAMB WAVE

*"The VOICE OF THE LORD IS
OVER THE WATERS;
the God of glory THUNDERS"*

– Psalm 29:3

As I draw the various data points of this book to a close, I hope that we can figuratively recognize the brilliant dream of God for humanity, one from which He will not be dissuaded. History may seem like a long series of delays, but much that has been hidden should be better understood within the mysteries, timing and sovereign purpose of God. On the other hand, those eschatological promises typified in Israel's possession of the Promised Land suggest that God's willingness to delay is in part related to our willingness to fully believe. His sovereign patience will wait for the Promised Land until that generation of faith arises.

> **"For good news came to us just as to them, but the message they heard did not benefit them, because they were not united by faith with those who listened."** (Hebrews 4:2)

I assure you, such a generation will be comprised of thoroughly new covenant people devoted to an unmixed gospel. Moses *cannot* take the Promised Land, only Joshua (Hebrew *'Yeshua'*; Greek, *Jesus'*).

So it will be in our day. We will rely on the Spirit more than ever and put no confidence in the flesh. We will need help, so for certain; God will help us. Even now, He is stirring His people to press into faith. He is expanding our focus on the Lordship of Jesus and our capacity to be fascinated by His beauty. We are hearing the call to flee Babylon's intoxications while receiving new vision to **"behold the Lamb of God who takes away the sins of the world"** (John 1:29).

Indeed, we *do* need help. One profound supply of infinite grace by which the Father will reveal His Son to us is in rediscovering the deeper potential of Communion. Especially as Evangelicals, if we give ourselves to a steady diet of bread and wine with real time for reflection, meditation and conversation with the Spirit of Christ, we will likely find new spiritual territories opening up in the landscape of our souls. The Holy Spirit longs to manifest Jesus, and there is so much more to reveal than we have known. Oh, to see and proclaim Christ and Him crucified. That was Paul's singular message.

Heaven stands ready to answer our pursuit. Packages of devotional and pastoral revelation are ready to be deployed to millions of people for whom the blood and bread gain priority.

But there are massive cosmic implications, as well. I believe we will begin to see and partake of Communion not just as remembrance, but *as reenactment of the Lamb's victory on the cross*. In chapters four and five, I likened the peril of God's nearness to sinful humans under the old covenant to an armed nuclear bomb placed in a refugee camp. Have you ever seen videos of nuclear bombs being tested? The release of power is almost unimaginable. Massive shockwaves blast outward from ground zero with devastating force. There is nothing like it.

Or is there?

If we can begin to see it, I believe each time we raise the body and blood, we release another munition of the triumph of Christ over Satan. Listen, we do not *recreate* that victory. It is His alone. But I believe one of the functions of Communion is that we are meant to *reenact* it, thereby practicing the agency of our future rulership with Christ as heirs and co-heirs (Romans 8:16-17,

Galatians 4:7). Would you like to participate in the eschatological certainty of Satan's final humiliation and defeat? Take Communion and boast in the glory of the cross. The presence of God that was (crudely put) thermonuclear in its danger is now touchable and tastable in the Bread of Presence and the Wine of Blood. When we consume it, we become receptacles of His triumph and trophies of His grace, therefore harbingers of Lucifer's doom.

Boom!

Each time we drink, each crumb we share, let us corporately prophecy the fall of Babylon, the overthrow of Antichrist, the glory of the Lamb who was slain, and the final binding of Satan at the end of the age. By virtue of our redeemed imagination, let us lean into the full manifestation of the risen Son's interplanetary, cosmic glory. How can such a holy, unfathomable God become food to us? I don't know, but that doesn't mean I don't want to eat! When we feast on Him, we not only "proclaim the Lord's death" until He comes, we joyfully and deliberately exult both in His humble, redemptive first coming, and His glorious, victorious second.

Tsunami Signals Sweeping Global Revival?

I want to give you a sense of how near the "Great Communion Blood Revival" might be. Sometimes we spend so much time believing that we resist the fulfillment when it comes because we had more faith to ask for the thing than to receive it. In the epic sci-fi movie, *Dune*, which reintroduced Frank Herbert's wildly popular novel to a new audience, a character named Shadout Mapes captures that challenge. The book presents a messianic figure who has been predicted and anticipated for thousands of years by countless oracles. But in the early days of his appearance, Shadout Mapes has trouble believing that the days of fulfillment might truly have arrived. She breathlessly exclaims, *"When one has lived with prophecy for so long, the moment of revelation is a shock."*

I want to shock you. Literally, with shockwaves.

First, we need to register that God often signals His intentions. That is part of the prophetic function of Scripture and the gifts of prophecy given by the Holy Spirit. In the last days, God promises **"wonders in the heavens above and signs on the earth below"** (Acts 2:19).

What is a sign, if not an alert system, a pointer? Look here! God gives wonders in heaven and signs on earth for a reason. While heavenly phenomena may not be common, that is out of necessity for the sign to have its intended impact. The record of their use is still significant enough to ask whether God would continue to use such signs today in the pattern of other momentous events: from the Star of Bethlehem, to the great, unusual darkness of the ninth plague on Egypt, to Joshua's long day, Hezekiah's sundial, and the darkness and earthquake that occurred during Jesus' crucifixion. All of these involved abnormalities of expected behavior. Each signaled a major development in God's plan.

Now let me tell you about Rick Ridings, a friend of mine and well-regarded leader in the Body of Christ. As founder and director of Succat Hallel House of Prayer in Jerusalem, Rick's reputation is that of a humble man and a sincere follower of Jesus, one not given to hyperbole or spiritual melodramatics. Below, I recount an open vision Rick was shown (only partially) beginning in February, 2012, then repeated with new details in April, 2014, which then recurred again with greater intensity and clarity years later in October, 2021. In sharing this, I want us to take note of a connection between his vision and a surprising natural fulfillment, and the uniquely confirming insight it affords us. Rick publicized this word on his website.[51]

> "I saw the Lord with a rod in His hand. He was standing over the International Date Line, near the Solomon Islands in the Pacific Ocean, which would indicate a change of "times and seasons." He took the staff and struck it forcefully against the ocean floor. This produced a spiritual tsunami of a huge wave of light that was headed towards Jerusalem and the Middle East.
>
> I saw many intercessors and harvesters who began to ride the tsunami wave. They were from the Pacific, especially from New Zealand, Australia, the Philippines, and Japan.

Rick went on to describe how the "wave" swept intercessors and harvesters from east to west, gathering them from Korea, China, Indonesia, Singapore, Malaysia, and India. He continued:

> "I saw that Satan had long feared that this wave would come, and that he had spent centuries to build one sea wall after another sea wall as barriers to try to stop this coming tsunami. Each seawall was a spiritual stronghold, with a demonic principality sitting on a throne on top of that seawall. The principality on each

throne had its arms crossed as if to show, "You will never get past me." But the tsunami wave (and earthquakes) broke down wall after wall.

These walls and "thrones" were "strongholds of Shintoism and idolatry…Buddhism and ancestor worship…and Hinduism." Each crumbled and fell before the wave as a great harvest of people were brought into the Kingdom of God. The fourth and final wall was that of Islam. This wall had a huge principality on its throne that looked very intimidating. But even that wall fell before this wave. There was a great 'breaking up of the fountains of the deep' that released even more water into this desert region, and the water levels rose quickly. This led to the gathering in of a great harvest.

Rick said he heard the voice of the Lord proclaiming loudly: "I am breaking up the fountains of the deep so that the earth may be covered with the glory of the Lord."

However, even though the 2021 vision was clear, the full timeline had unfolded over many years, leaving Rick somewhat discouraged. Given the apparent absence of any literal or spiritual tsunami as he had seen in the vision, Rick asked the Lord for a sign that the word was true.

Once again, it added up to 2022.

Beloved, something began that year.

On January 15, 2022, a volcanic eruption off the island nation of Tonga completely caught scientists by surprise by triggering *two* types of tsunamis: "classic" tsunamis caused by the displacement of large volumes of water, and meteotsunamis caused by fast-moving pressure disturbances in the atmosphere. These "atmospheric waves" created faster than normal water waves.

Wonders in the Heavens Above

Though similar words have been received and given by others – after all, the whole earth is groaning for great revival – something about Rick's word stood out to me as uniquely important. I was so intrigued that I dug in for more information, only to find myself shocked at how the Lord seemed to be using this word to confirm our team's many dreams about the Great Communion Blood Revival.

Here's a sampling of official news reports and scientific studies from around the world. Take a moment and read them.

- "On January 15, 2022…in the South Pacific Kingdom of Tonga, an undersea volcano called Hunga Tonga Hunga Ha'apai began to erupt violently…(which then) surprised scientists by triggering two types of tsunamis: 'classic' tsunamis caused by the displacement of large volumes of water, and meteotsunamis caused by fast-moving pressure disturbances in the atmosphere. These 'atmospheric waves' created faster than normal waves"[52]

- "Not since the 1883 eruption of the Indonesian volcano Krakatoa have scientists had the opportunity to study, in real time, an event so large that it literally sent shock waves across the globe… The tsunami spread from the volcano and traveled across the Pacific Ocean at the speed of an airliner – approximately 450 miles per hour, typical of ocean-spanning tsunamis…but a pressure wave released by the eruption traveled even faster – about 700 miles per hour – raising smaller tsunamis in bodies of water as far away as the Caribbean and

Mediterranean seas. Where the pressure wave passed the deep water at trenches it moved water at about the same speed as it travelled creating (an even) larger tsunami" through a particular phenomena of resonance.[53]

- "This explosion was heard in various parts of the world, like Samoa and New Zealand (more than 2000 km away from the eruption point), and…in a series of audible bangs as far as Alaska. Also, an atmospheric shock-wave propagated around the globe, whose associated pressure disturbances were measured by weather stations" from New Zealand to Europe.[54]

the unique dynamics of this event occurred because heaven and earth came into a resonance

This particular type of resonance occurs when coupled water waves grow rapidly *because the speed of the atmospheric wave matches the natural speed of a tsunami wave.* Let me say that differently, the unique dynamics of this event occurred *because heaven and earth came into a resonance…*or "sonic agreement."

Moving at 300 meters per second, the "atmospheric waves created faster than normal water waves." In effect, heaven pushed the water across the Pacific far faster than expected.

Here's the kicker. That particular type of atmospheric activity has an official, scientific name.

It's called a *Lamb Wave*.

- "The fastest of these atmospheric waves were a type of pressure wave called a Lamb wave (named after English mathematician, Horace Lamb). Strong Lamb waves in the atmosphere are uncommon and are usually associated with events that release tremendous amounts of energy… The first Lamb Waves to radiate away from the eruption traveled about 710 mph…surround(ing) the globe and eventually circling it three-and-a-half times."[55]

The power and magnitude of this event left scientists somewhat at a loss for superlatives, as they had little to compare it to. The Tonga eruption was simply in a class all by itself. In essence, the eruption was so intense it caused the atmosphere to ring like a bell. Measuring sound waves around the world, they said that what happened in this eruption at the International Dateline was so strong that a Lamb wave shot around the world *three times*. It could not be heard by the human ear except as a sort of sonic boom, but scientists said it was far more powerful than a sonic boom.

I encourage you, right now, google the words "Tonga", "volcano", "eruption", "tsunami" and "2022." Watch videos of the astonishing satellite imagery that captured this truly massive, global event (links in this footnote[56]).

What Does it Mean

Firstly, to see the Lord standing at the International Dateline means Rick was witnessing the point on earth where one day changes to another day, where *today becomes tomorrow*. The rod of the Lord struck at the place where time resets.

The Great Communion Revival

As I said at the beginning, we are in a new era.

Next, located immediately to the west of the International Date Line, Tonga is the first nation to greet the new day. Sweeping west, if we form a line "as the crow flies" from Tonga to Jerusalem, Fiji and the Solomon Islands come next. Even as "Solomon's House" filled with the glory of the Lord, **"the earth will be filled with the knowledge of the glory of the LORD as the waters cover the sea."** (Habakkuk 2:14). This is what Rick saw.

The result of the eruption was not only unprecedented in scope, it was measurable *by the sound it released*. Satellite videos reveal the sound appearing to sweep the skies clean as atmospheric Lamb waves pulled and pushed the liquid energy of the tsunami faster than it should have gone.

Quite possibly, that event had already been decreed in a prophetic vision from an intercessor in Jerusalem. The resulting resonance was so powerful it sent shockwaves around the entire planet three times.

Three, the number of resurrection.

The Lamb's Wave.

To my knowledge, Rick had no idea that the Tongas have been contending for revival for many years, even calling themselves the "Womb of the Dawn" nation after Psalm 110. Nor did he know of the "Deep Sea Canoe" vision that believers on the Solomon Islands have been praying into for nearly 40 years, involving a tsunami that would begin in their region, sweeping west and east, and converging with massive revival on Jerusalem.[57]

Could a "Lamb Wave" truly be ready to sweep the earth?

chapter 12

GLOBAL COMMUNION

"There is a fountain filled with blood
DRAWN FROM EMMANUEL'S VEINS
And sinners plunged beneath that flood
LOSE ALL THEIR GUILTY STAINS."

– William Cowper (1731-1800)

A global invitation to Evangelicals, Pentecostals and Charismatics to reengage Christ around Communion

Could we, the global Body of Christ, from every corner and continent, comprised of confessing Christians from the many Protestant denominations around the world, along with our Roman Catholic and Orthodox brothers, or any who subscribe to the Apostle's Creed (or the similar Creed of Faith for Coptics) commit to a decade of Eucharistic focus?

As I have already stated, my appeal is mostly to countless Evangelical, Charismatic, Protestant, Reformed, Bible Churches and Non-Denominational fellowships who would be moved by God to engage in Communion with a sacred attentiveness beyond our historic routines.

Immediately below, I suggest five areas for corporate and personal creativity, inspiration and, dare I say, experimentation in an attempt to expand the focus we place upon Communion. In addition, these five areas are followed by eight recommendations to assist with practical implementation. In the grace of God, I believe the sum total could produce enduring fruitfulness among us beyond our current measure:

Five Areas in Which to Renew the Experience of Communion

1. Physical Healing & Emotional Renewal[58]
2. Fellowship with Other Believers
3. A Witness to the Lost
4. Reenactment of Christ's Triumph
5. Proclamation of His Soon Return

Eight Recommendations for How to Meaningfully Partake

1. Practice three *"Beholdings"* of the Lamb of God

   - **Behold the Man** (or *behold His hands*). This is our inward beholding of Him. We set our gaze upon His body at the Last Supper, prior the cross, on the cross, and after the cross, as a form of worshipful meditation for the price He paid as an act of love.

   - **Behold the Blood.** This is our prayer to God for more revelation of the mysteries of Christ and the power of His blood on our behalf. When we behold the blood, we put ourselves into the epic story of Passover with deeply personal reflections on our own redemption from the bondage of sin and death.

   - **"Behold the Lamb!"** We make this proclamation in a spirit of appeal to God to extend His mercy and love to the lost and the broken. Literally, we are saying, "Father, behold the Lamb, your Son, who takes away the sins of the world," invoking the mercies of God upon the world through the precious blood of Christ.

2. **Take Communion personally with a commitment to overthrowing accusation in your heart.** Forgive *everyone* for *everything*. Cancel their debts to you. Free them from debtors' prison, and free yourself in the process. Heap blessings on your enemies. Do not excuse this imperative, or somehow justify your unique right to hold onto grudges and bitterness. Apply and

confess verses describing the righteousness Christ has imputed to you. Do not condemn others, nor live under condemnation.

3. Practice the Disciples' Prayer as a conversational form of Communion. Rediscover the rhythm and grace of the prayer, along with its authority. Turn it into worship and dialogue with God. Every word matters. In particular, when you cannot take Communion, practice the Disciples' Prayer as if it were bread and wine in your mouth.

4. Celebrate Communion with your family. Train them to bless, not curse. Turn off Netflix and have a once-a-week family night around Communion. Read any of the passages mentioned in this book, especially those involving Passover or the Passion Week, then talk to each other about any new insights you discover. Take Communion with your spouse. Practice the "Three Beholdings" with your children.

5. Join with others in home groups to seek greater understanding of the new covenant. Again, practice the "Three Beholdings" with your friends, but also determine to dig deep into the meat of the Word together. Leave the milk behind. Ask the Lord for a spirit of wisdom and revelation to become mature, new covenant sons and daughters of the Most High. Pray together, and pray the power of the blood and name of Jesus until you begin to see the fruit of those prayers.

6. Set aside times for corporate focus and boasting in high praise with particular focus on the blood of Jesus. Pastors, boldly and creatively disrupt your Sunday schedule to build a different sort of church culture that more obviously esteems the blood of Jesus. Experiment with monthly gatherings where you not only take Communion together, but you spend the entire service in communion with God and one another. Make it a meal. Make it worship. Make it special. Make it joyful. Be extravagant and even wasteful in the time you give to extended periods of high praise, liturgical reflection, biblical teaching, and corporate prayer regarding the triumph of Christ and the mercy of His blood.

7. Pray for Israel to come to the full realization of Jesus as their Messiah out of their own prophetic history. The drama of the Passover is a permanent testimony to the fact that salvation is to the Jew first (Romans 1:16). The weighty lessons of the blood has been their gift to us, so pray for Israel to awaken to the very oracles God first entrusted to them. Pray for the Jewish people's eyes to open. Pray "Behold the Lamb" prayers over the entire nation.

8. Share your insights with others. Are you learning new things? Share them! Practice the vernacular of grace and the wonders of redemption in holy conversation. Immerse yourself in study of the cross of Christ, the Passover lamb, the scarlet thread of redemption and the many types and symbols. Turn those moments into listening moments with the Holy Spirit, then share the riches with others. Quit speaking ill of other churches, or brothers and sisters, but bless instead. When we feed each other in this way, we multiply the Bread of Life among us.

For more on the Great Communion Revival
visit deanbriggs.com/gcr

For more information about Dean Briggs Ministries visit deanbriggs.com

---

APOSTOLIC FOUNDATIONS SERIES
- Filmed in high resolution
- Lifetime Personal License
- Free Study Guide
- Free Companion Booklet

Total Superiority of the New Covenant

58 sessions (10 hours total)
7-12 minutes each

Power of Your New Creation Life

60 sessions (11+ hours total)
7-15 minutes each

Calling & Purpose of the Ekklesia

64 sessions (14 hours total)
Avg. session length: 13 min

END NOTES

[1] "We should give special attention to typology (as) a major category of prophecy." — Robertson McQuilkin, *Understanding and Applying the Bible* (Moody, Chicago) 1983, expanded ed. 2009

[2] Jonathan Gottschall, *The Storytelling Animal: How Stories Make Us Human* (Houghton Mifflin Harcourt, Boston) 2012; p. 11

[3] *Taking God Seriously: Vital Things We Need to Know* (InterVarsity Press, Westmont) 1994

[4] Walter Wink, *Engaging the Powers: Discernment and Resistance in a World of Domination* (Fortress Press, Minneapolis) 1992

[5] Get my free course on dreams: "Drop Zones & Thin Spaces" at go.deanbriggs.com/dreams

[6] *Les Misérables* (Simon and Schuster, New York) 2005, p. 243

[7] https://www.wsj.com/articles/the-coronavirus-pandemic-will-forever-alter-the-world-order-11585953005

[8] Some maintain that Abraham's three visitors were really angels in the appearance of men. But Genesis 18:1 is clear: it was "the LORD" (Yahweh) who appeared to Abraham. Similarly, it is Yahweh who speaks in verses 13, 20, 26, and 33 and Abraham stands "before the LORD" in verse 22.

[9] Exo. 32:14, Deut 9:5-6, Lev. 26:42

[10] *The Divine Conspiracy: Rediscovering Our Hidden Life in God* (HarperSanFrancisco, San Francisco) 1998. In a treatment of this work called *Theology of Dallas Willard: Discovering Protoevangelical Faith,* Dr. Gary Black explored how both the right and the left tend to undermine the gospel as Jesus taught it. The right tends to turn the gospel into "vampire faith" (preferring the redemptive virtue of Jesus's blood to relationship with Jesus Himself) while subtly distorting God's nature through an obsessively granular substitutionary atonement framework. Meanwhile, the leftward gospel is largely a force for activism and "self-determined acts of righteousness" (149). The right focuses on good beliefs, the left on good behaviors. Black, (Wipf and Stock Publishers, Eugene) 2018

[11] "No one may see Me and live" was declared by God *after* the Law was ratified, not before. (Exodus 33:20, NIV)

[12] *Longhairs Rising* (Champion Press, Kansas City) 2018, p. 41-42

[13] At least in part, this represents the spirit of my appeal in the final chapter for the corporate identity of the Body of Christ to become defined (rather than divided) by our mutual experience of Communion as the corporate, blood-bought nation of Christ.

[14] tagline for series, *Clive Barker's Books of Blood: Volume I-3* (Berkley Books, New York) 1986

[15] *The Passover Prophecies: How God is Realigning Hearts and Nations in Crisis* (Charisma House, Lake Mary) 2020, p. 52

[16] Rabbi Aaron L. Raskin, "Pey (Fey): The seventeenth letter of the Hebrew alphabet" (https://www.chabad.org/library/article_cdo/aid/137089/jewish/Pey-Fey.htm)

[17] *Judaism as Creed and Life* (Macmillan, New York) 1922, p. 225

[18] Mordecai M. Kaplan, *The New Haggadah For the Pesah Seder* (New York, Behrman House) 1941, p. 50-51

[19] *Honor the Blood* (Osterhus Publishing House, Minneapolis)

[20] *Heroes, Hero-Worship, and the Heroic in History* (James Fraser, London), 1841

[21] "The Test of Blood" by Rabbi Alex Israel (https://www.alexisrael.org/pesach---blood-on-the-doorposts)

[22] Even John struggled. He "marveled" at the sight of her. The Greek word thaumazō means to wonder, and by implication, to admire (Jesus "marveled" at the centurion's faith, Matt. 8:10, and the crowds marveled when Jesus cast out a demon, Matt. 9:33). In other words, John was tempted to be more amazed than repulsed. More attracted then disgusted.

[23] Entry on Rev. 18:4, *The Expositor's Bible Commentary*. Edited by Tremper Longman III and David E. Garland. (Zondervan, Grand Rapids) 1990

[24] Johann Wolfgang von Goethe, "Faust," in *Goethe: The Collected Works*, edited by Matthew Bell, vol. 2 (Princeton University Press, Princeton) 2019

[25] "In the traditional western interpretation it has been argued that the enemy in the individual lament of Psalm 59 is no more than an unbeliever and a traitor. However, an afro-centric interpretation of the Psalm reveals that this adversary shares various traits with the contemporary African witch." Attempting a fresh translation of the Psalm, Kotzé eliminates "later additions to the text that obscure the nature of this Psalm"as a sort of righteous incantation against witches and shamans who utilize the power of blood for evil purposes. The first two verses thus become:

1. "Defend me against my enemies, my God; protect me against those who rise up against me.
2. *Defend me against the workers of power, and rescue me from the men of blood."*

Z. Kotzé, "The Witch in Psalm 59: An Afro-centric Interpretation"; January 2008, *Old Testament Essays* 21(2):383-390

[26] Thomas W. Jacobson, M.A., and Wm. Robert Johnston, Ph.D.; available at http://media.wix.com/ugd/cacd2b_7806916e82d547378e78f74fb3dd9383.pdf

[27] "Amon" Brittanica Online; https://www.britannica.com/topic/Amon

[28] "Sacrificing a Lamb in Egypt" by Jan Assmann, Professor Emeritus of Egyptology, University of Heidelberg and Dr. Rabbi Zev Farber; https://www.thetorah.com/article/sacrificing-a-lamb-in-egypt

[29] The official Jewish Aramaic translation of the Torah, considered authoritative

[30] *Guide for the Perplexed, Part III, Ch. XLVI* by Moses Maimonides, trans. M. Friedländer (1904); (https://www.sacred-texts.com/jud/gfp/gfp182.htm)

[31] Dr. Douglas Petrovich makes a fascinating and well-considered case that Amenhotep II (c. 1455-1418 BC) is the more legitimate candidate for pharaoh of the Exodus, not the later Ramses II (c. 1303-1213 BC) as many have assumed. If true, then Amenhotep II's great grandson, Akhenaten (husband to the famous Queen Nefertitilf) assumed the throne only 65 years after the events of the Exodus had devastated Egypt's economy, military, religion and social fabric. For the purpose of this chapter, what I find most compelling about that possibility is that a singularly unique event happened during Akhenaten's reign that possibly confirmed the critical damage done to the reputation of Egypts gods: Akhenaten became the first pharaoh to declare that Egypt would only worship one God, not many. This supreme god would no longer be Amun-Ra, but a related deity called Aton.

Prior this, Egypt had been famously, proudly and profoundly polytheistic for over 1600 years of dynastic devotion to many gods. What would cause a pharaoh to risk subverting the legacy of his forefathers unless a national trauma of truly historic proportions had occurred within the span of his immediate family's memory, from which the nation had likely spent decades in recovery mode, and which perhaps still continued to negatively impact his own rule? Whether you were a thoughtful ruler, or a superstitious one, would this not cast obvious doubts on the strength of Egypt's pantheon and make you question your loyalty to it?

Regardless, the traditions of Egypt proved too strong, as his famous son Tutankhamun (King Tut) dismantled all of his father's reforms. Petrovich, Douglas N. (2006). Amenhotep II and the Historicity of the Exodus-Pharaoh. The Master's Seminary Journal, 17:1, 1-30.

[32] Charitie Lees Bancroft (1841-1923); public domain

[33] *Christians in the Age of Outrage: How to Bring Our Best When the World Is at Its Worst* (Tyndale House Publishers, Carol Stream) 2018

[34] L. E. Modesitt, Jr, *Gravity Dreams* (Tor Books, New York) 1999, ch. 10

[35] Mark 16:19; Acts 2:33; 1 Pet. 3:22

[36] *Mere Christianity* (HarperOne, San Francisco) 1952

[37] Silence is a part of cancelling accusation. Contrary to carnal instinct, it nullifies the strength of the accuser to offer no reply. Similarly, a major emphasis of fasting is to "take away the yoke from your midst, the pointing of the finger, and speaking wickedness" (Isaiah 58:6,9). Interestingly, the Hebrew word for fast literally means "to cover the mouth."

[38] Isaiah 53:7 (cf. Acts 8:32) ; John 1:29 ; Rev. 5:12

[39] Briggs, (Champion Press, Kansas City) 2018, p. 43-44

[40] *The Cost of Discipleship* (Touchstone, New York) 1959, p. 88

[41] Marisa J. Lapish, "The Eucharist as Iconic Experience of Divine Love: Ancient-Future Orienteering with Julian of Norwich" (https://kenarchy.org/wp-content/uploads/2022/10/Kenarchy_Volume4.4.pdf)

[42] Words and music by Andrea Marie Reagan, Brandon Hampton, Brock Human, Michael Ketterer, Will Reagan; United Pursuit Music (Admin. by Capitol CMG Publishing) CCLI Song #7047290

[43] Notes at Exo. 25:23-30, Lev. 24:5-9; *The Jewish Study Bible*; Jewish Publication Society (2004); Oxford University Press, Inc.

[44] *Celebration of Discipline: The Path to Spiritual Growth* (Harper and Row, New York City), 1978.

[45] *Hearing God: Developing a Conversational Relationship with God*; (InterVarsity Press, Westmont) 1999, p. 133-134

[46] "It is our duty to adore the Blessed Sacrament…not only do we not sin by adoring, we do sin by not adoring." Augustine of Hippo, "Sermons on the First Epistle of John" (Sermon 227), in *The Nicene and Post-Nicene Fathers: First Series, vol. 7*, ed. Philip Schaff and Henry Wace. (Hendrickson Publishers, Peabody) 2004

[47] "Baptism and Growth in Communion; Report of the Lutheran-Roman Catholic Commission on Unity" ed. Prof. Dr Dirk Lange (The Lutheran World Federation, Pontifical Council for Promoting Christian Unity, 2022); viewable at https://issuu.com/portaluteranos/docs/baptism_and_growth_in_communion

[48] Lest one think Ignatius was a Romanist or a legalist, he also wrote in the *Letter to the Magnesians*, "Do not be deceived by strange teachings, nor with old fables, which are unprofitable. For if we still live according to Jewish Law, we acknowledge that we have not received grace."

[49] "First Apology," in *The Ante-Nicene Fathers: Translations of the Writings of the Fathers down to A.D. 325, vol. 1*, ed. Alexander Roberts and James Donaldson (Hendrickson Publishers, Peabody) 2004

[50] "Frederick Buechner Quote of the Day," August 1, 2018; originally published in *Wishful Thinking*.

[51] "Spiritual Tsunami from the South Pacific and Asia Towards the Middle East" (https://succathallel.com/spiritual-vision-tsunami)

[52] "In depth: Surprising tsunamis caused by explosive eruption in Tonga"; US Geological Survey official website (https://www.usgs.gov/centers/pcmsc/news/depth-surprising-tsunamis-caused-explosive-eruption-tonga)

[53] "Massive Volcanic Eruption and Tsunami Informs Plan for Future Eruptions, Sea-level Rise"; ibid (https://www.usgs.gov/news/featured-story/massive-volcanic-eruption-and-tsunami-informs-plan-future-eruptions-sea-level)

[54] "Abbrescia, M., Avanzini, C., Baldini, L. *et al*. Observation of Rayleigh-Lamb waves generated by the 2022 Hunga-Tonga volcanic eruption with the POLA detectors at Ny-Ålesund. *Sci Rep* 12, 19978 (2022). https://doi.org/10.1038/s41598-022-23984-2

[55] Same as footnote 51

[56] See deanbriggs.com/gcr for footage compiled from 1. https://d9-wret.s3.us-west-2.amazonaws.com/assets/palladium/production/s3fs-public/media/video/Tonga tsunami HD_final (1).mp4 *(notice the timing of the eruption right as day turns to night at the International Date Line)*

   2. https://www.youtube.com/watch?v=AcFropu7uWw

   3. https://www.youtube.com/watch?v=zMgvibBP710

[57] "The Deep Sea Canoe Vision" by Rev. Michael Maeliau, Solomon Islands, 1986 (https://www.ipcprayer.org/ipc-connections/item/5050-the-deep-sea-canoe-vision.html)

[58] "Another function of the human blood is its capacity to bring healing to the physical body. Human blood is composed of more than just red blood cells. In fact, over half (55 percent) of our blood is not red at all. It is a clear liquid, known as plasma, that is 92 percent water. The other 8 percent includes many essential substances necessary to keep our bodies healthy. These are proteins, hormones, vitamins, enzymes and salts. Should the body become ill, the blood alters its normals to adjust and promote healing. The white blood cells (leucocytes) are the body's first line of defense against bacterial invaders. When bacteria enter the body, white blood cells are produced in great numbers. They travel to the infection and engulf the invaders. The blood of Jesus spiritually does the same for the body of Christ. When Satan invades, the Holy Spirit stands ready to come to our aid and bring the needed healing. The Lord desires that we walk in divine health. If we stay in close communion with Him, we will find our spiritual man will not become sick and depleted, needing continual healing. Satan tries to drain us of our spiritual strength and weaken us to the point where we have no resistance against His attacks. Staying in the flow of God's Spirit prevents this, as we then have His strength to overcome and walk victoriously." — Betty Miller, "What the Bible Says About the Blood of Jesus", https://bibleresources.org/the-blood-of-jesus/)